LIKE A LILY AMONG THORNS

SAINT SHENOUDA PRESS

LIKE A LILY AMONG THORNS

GIRLS GUIDE TO HOLY WEEK READINGS

Rebecca Kozman

ST SHENOUDA PRESS
SYDNEY, AUSTRALIA
2020

LIKE A LILY AMONG THORNS
Girls Guide to Holy Week Readings

Rebecca Kozman

COPYRIGHT © 2020
St. Shenouda Press

ST SHENOUDA PRESS
8419 Putty Rd
Putty, NSW, 2330
Australia

www.stshenoudapress.com

ISBN 13: 978-0-6485754-7-4

Contents

PALM SUNDAY   9

MONDAY EVE   13

HOLY MONDAY   27

TUESDAY EVE   43

HOLY TUESDAY   57

WEDNESDAY EVE   73

HOLY WEDNESDAY   87

THURSDAY EVE   101

GREAT THURSDAY   115

FRIDAY EVE   135

GOOD FRIDAY   151

BRIGHT SATURDAY   169

*"But Jesus answered them saying,
"The hour has come that the Son
of Man should be glorified.""*
John 12:23

Introduction

Do you know that time during the Pascha service when the deacon is singing the Psalm slowly before the Gospel giving the people the chance to contemplate on the psalm and the gospel reading? I hope and pray that this book will help you to contemplate during this time.

By the grace of God, this book will provide you with an explanation of the readings of Holy Week. The readings of the prophecies, Psalms, and Gospels have been arranged to "hang together." One of the joys of Passion Week is discovering all these links and seeing how they help us to deepen our understanding when we put it all together. Each hour will delve into different contemplations of each reading, taking us on a journey to better understand and appreciate the final days of our Lord Christ; from His triumphant entry into Jerusalem to His Joyous Resurrection.

Now, this isn't a "girly" book, but there are messages in the readings of this week I want you to see as women of God. May this book enlighten our minds and open our hearts, and may God grant you an abundance of blessings through this Holy Week.

PALM SUNDAY & GENERAL FUNERAL SERVICE

"Hosanna in the Highest, This is the King of Israel. Blessed is he who comes in the Name of the Lord of Hosts!"

Please read this the night before Palm Sunday so you can enjoy the Liturgy and experience His presence while understanding the happenings and taking time for your own contemplation.

As I began writing this book, Orthodox Churches have been attacked and bombings were held in Egypt; all on Palm Sunday. More than a dozen people dead, and even more injured. A friend shared a beautiful contemplation at the time – "As they were saying 'He who sits upon the Cherubim,' they had suddenly found themselves in front of Him! How beautiful is it, when they [the martyrs] were singing 'Evlogimenos' ('Hosanna in the Highest') and receiving their King, that they did not know that in fact, the King Himself was receiving them in the Heavenly Kingdom!" May these martyrs intercede on our behalf and remember us before our Lord.

As we welcome the King into Jerusalem, we also accept Him in our hearts and lives. We are welcoming a new life in Christ. Palm Sunday summons us to behold our King; The Word of God made flesh. We are called to behold Him not simply as the One who came to us riding on a colt, but as the One who is always present in His Church, coming ceaselessly to us in every prayer, every sacrament, and in every act of love. Christ liberates us from the darkness of sin and the bondage of death.

I will begin this explanation with a quick overview of the prayers before the Liturgy held on Palm Sunday. The Church makes a procession of twelve areas around the Church, similar to the one made during the Feast of the Cross, with a Gospel reading read at each station in front of an icon to commemorate a saint. During the matins prayer, there is a procession inside the altar, indicating that our lives as believers start by God's plan. During the Liturgy, the four Gospels are read, each one facing a different direction as the fulfilment of the prophecy that the Gospel will be preached to all four corners of the Earth. These readings announce the beginning of Christ's Kingdom and outline the conditions of acceptance into His Kingdom. While on the doorstep of passion, one will not be able to travel the Lord's road unless they place in their heart that their soul must bear fruit of the Holy Spirit, leaving hypocrisy and outward appearances which brings nothing but people's praise.

The joy expressed is neither complete nor consistent. The Pharisees envied Him and the love the people had for Him. When His children cried out "Hosanna", the Jewish leaders questioned Him, "By what authority are

You doing these things?" (Matt. 21:23). It is even these people who welcomed Him who would soon reject Him a few days later; "Crucify Him, crucify Him!" (Luke 23:21). Such an ironic theme is expressed throughout the entire week. After entering Jerusalem, Christ went into the temple of God and drove out all those who bought and sold in the temple. The "temple" is our hearts, our minds, and our lives. When we were baptised, Christ in Spirit came into us and became one in us. Therefore, when He sees that you are filled with the love of money and doves are being sold in the temple of your heart, He barges in and turns the tables. He comes into your heart and flips everything upside down.

Do you not know that "you are God's temple, and His Spirit dwells in you? If anyone destroys their temple, God will destroy him. For God's temple is holy, and you are that temple" (1 Cor. 3:16-17). You have taken away the opportunity for worshippers to lift their hearts to God in prayer in the designated Holy Place. You have made the Divine temple a marketplace for human gain. Does Christ then not have the right to interfere with the temple and drive away everything He hates and everything that is destroying it? He did it for the salvation of the Jews, and for our salvation too. Clean your temple this week – don't be like the Pharisees who appear clean on the outside, yet their cups are not clean on the inside.

Palm Sunday is the day of happiness and the beginning of the week of sorrows. We enter the Church dressedup, with palm leaves and singing hymns of joy, but we leave draped in sorrow and mourning.

The General Funeral Service is conducted at the end of

the Liturgy. During Passion Week, there is no incense raised for the departed, thus why the Church provides this service – for the souls that depart during these holy days. This service is performed by the priest praying on the water before the altar, with which he then blesses the people.

Resurrection has overcome death. The first words of the whole week are Ezekiel 37:1-14. This passage assures us that the crucified life in Christ raises to life those who were dead through sin, though they had become dry bones. The Church addresses these words to us: "I shall put my spirit in you, and you shall live...I will cover you with flesh and skin and put breath in you and you shall live" (Ezek. 37:6). This theme is seen throughout the whole Bible.

The best way to start Holy Week is with no evil in your heart so that you can benefit from these holy days. Reconcile with your brothers and sisters:

"All this is from God, who through Christ reconciled us to Himself and gave us the ministry of reconciliation; that is, in Christ God was reconciling the world to Himself, not counting their trespasses against them, and entrusting to us the message of reconciliation."

+ 2 Corinthians 5:18-19 +

Monday Eve

Preparation

FIRST HOUR
PREPARE FOR HIS SUFFERING

| Zeph. 1:2-12 | Ps. 26:6-8 | John 12:20-36 |

The prophecy of the first hour from Zephaniah talks about Judah's lukewarmness towards the Lord and proclaims God's judgement of the nations in the Old Testament, *"I will consume man and beast..."* The Lord is showing the destruction that will fall on those who deny their Creator; saying that both man and beast will be consumed. If His people lose their holy life, He intends to consume the whole earth. God refuses to mix what is for Him and what is for the devil, and fellowship between light and darkness. Verse twelve shows God holding a lamp, searching the dark and hidden corners of Jerusalem so that no evil man would escape from His judgement. He uses the lamp to separate the wicked who insist on disregarding God. God does not threaten His people, but instead He warns them to be vigilant towards His commandments and they know the consequences of their actions.

The Psalm of this hour is a prophecy concerning baptism which is a declaration of war against the devil and his fallen angels. In baptism, Jesus Christ becomes our light and salvation, and with His help, we overcome these enemies in battle. Sing praises to Him, cry to Him with your voice, beg for His mercy, and seek Him – that way you will feel His help in your times of trouble – *"walk while you have the light, lest darkness overtake you... believe in the light that you may become sons of light"* (John 12:35-36).

Now – here is our connection to the New Testament. The first chapter of Zephaniah portrays God as though in the midst of Judah, the worshipper of idols, to judge it, whereas, in the final chapter, He proclaims His dwelling among mankind as a whole, to let them rejoice over Him as He does over them. In the New Testament, The Lord Jesus, wishing to be among the Jews, came to the temple in Jerusalem in daylight and stayed among them. That was when He cleared the temple. But as each hour turned into darkness, He evaluated everything around Him as though with a lamp and found no place to rest His head.

Have you ever been faced with a decision that involved God? For example, your friends invited you to a party, but you know that you have Bible Study and you are faced with a choice. The Lord wants us to choose Him just as He chose us to be His children. We need to remember that there will be a judgement day which we should always be preparing for. By walking in the light of God and His love and truth, we give God a place to rest within us and us in Him.

To conclude the first hour of Monday Eve, we see that through the prophecy of Zephaniah, the prophet is trying to warn Judah and Jerusalem about the destruction that will come upon the Babylonians and the last days. We see a similar warning by our Lord Jesus as He warns the people and disciples of the judgement that will also befall them in the last days, thus why they need to walk in the light. Now, this is not to scare us, but told in order for us to look forward to His coming so that we may finally be united with Him for eternity and become daughters of the Highest King.

THIRD HOUR
PREPARE FOR THE LAST DAYS

Zeph. 1:14-18	Zeph. 2:1-2	Ps. 28:9
	Luke 9:18-22	

The third hour contains two prophecies from Zephaniah the prophet, warning Judah and Jerusalem about the great day of the Lord. The great day of the Lord is a joyful wedding day for the believers who are prepared for it through the exalted riches of God's grace; and a day of wrath, distress, desolation, and gloominess for those who are not ready. The evildoers in the great day of the Lord, who walk in evil, oppose the truth and do not listen to the voice and the commandment of the Lord, will be like blind men, unable to enjoy the splendour of the glory of God. They will see God as a mighty Judge, and not as a heavenly Groom who grants His people the fellowship of glory with Him.

"Neither their silver nor their gold shall be able to deliver them in the day of the Lord's wrath…He will make speedy riddance of all those who dwell in the land" (Zeph. 1:18). Nothing materialistic you value will be able to protect you in the end. I wonder how those who foolishly carry such heavy loads of jewellery do not worry about death, and how they can be so consumed with worldly and materialistic things. It can be easy to fall into habits of gossiping and doing things behind other people's backs, but we should always be aware of how our actions and words can affect us and others. For the sake of our own salvation, we must always watch what we are doing and pray for others, even if they don't treat us the same way. Being watchful and prayerful helps us to prepare for the day when the Lord comes. We will only have one thing left in our hearts that the Lord loves – love.

"It is fitting for the women who minister to Christ, to adorn themselves, not with gold, but with the Word, through which, alone, the glitter of gold will shine."

+ *St. Clement of Alexandria* +

The Psalm is a plea to God that He saves His inheritance and becomes a Shepherd unto them. Question – why is it that the Old Testament prophecies mostly refer to Jerusalem and saving its people? Are they not the ones who rejected Christ as their King in the New Testament? Are they not the ones who were not ready to receive Him? That's why the prophecies were written, as a warning and chance for His selected people to repent and be ready for Him. When God saw that they were still not ready, He sent down His only begotten Son. Even David, a prophet and king, was crying to God in His holy sanctuary to save His people and to hold them up in His bosom as their Shepherd.

The Gospel of Luke that we read in this hour shows Christ asking His disciples who they think He is. He emphasises *"you"* when He asks them as a test of their faith. However, after He receives Peter's response, He *"strictly warned and commanded"* them to tell no one who He was and about Him – why? It simply was not His time; the prophecies were not yet fulfilled that He would be betrayed by His friend. However, Christ does repeat a prophecy that the Son of Man will suffer, be rejected, killed, and raised on the third day. Christ speaks in third person here again to test the faith of His disciples and to prepare them for His upcoming passion in the next few days. Jesus has taught us, through this, to watch and pray, a theme which will pop up a lot in the next few days.

SIXTH HOUR
ARE YOU READY?

Joel 1:5-15	Ps. 29:1-2	Mark 10:32-34

The prophecy read from Joel is heavy, so I'll only go into a few details that give you the big picture. The first verse is especially crucial; *"Awake, you drunkards, and weep; and wail..."*. Being drunkards by the wine of the love of this world, the people deny themselves the new wine; namely the Holy Spirit. Let the old Israel wail, because having rejected the dwelling of the Spirit, the new heavenly wine will be cut off their mouth. Let the new Israel, women of faith of the New Testament, rejoice; having rejected the wine of the world to enjoy the life-giving wine.

> *"Like fire consuming reeds, the pure tear would abolish every carnal and spiritual uncleanness…God does not need or want for a man [women] to weep and lament, but rather wish him [women] to rejoice, and have joy in His love."*
>
> + *St. John El-Dargi* +

Verse seven also stands out; *"He has laid waste My vine and ruined My fig tree"* (Monday of the Holy Pascha focuses on the fig tree, keep an eye out). The capitalisation of *'My'* here indicates that the Lord is speaking. The Lord calls His people His vine and fig tree; as the vine presents the grapes that, together with the Lord, pass through the wine-press, bear the features of His passion, and enter with Him to the power of His resurrection. And the fig, with its sweet outer cover that embraces a great number of tiny seeds, refers to the work, the love and unity of the sweet Holy Spirit, who embraces the members together. The sin makes the vine and the fig tree lose their distinctive feature; namely destroys the work of the crucified Christ and that of the Holy Spirit in us. God feels joy as He sees His people *"like grapes in the wilderness; as the first fruits on the fig tree in its first season"* (Hosea 9:10). Our aim is to be like that fruitful vine, working together and lifting each other up towards Him.

Now the Psalm; short yet powerful, like always. The context behind this Psalm is that David is warning the people to look away from themselves and look instead to the God of Israel. Although David refers to the people as *mighty ones,* he still encourages them to recognize the Lord God and to give unto Him *glory and strength.* How should they do this? By worshipping the Lord in the beauty of holiness. We should all bow in humble recognition of His greatness and surpassing beauty. His holy love, grace, justice, and majesty are all beautiful.

If you look at the first verse of this hour's Gospel, you will see that the disciples were *amazed* and *afraid.* Why? They sensed danger in their mission because Jesus was a wanted man. They were amazed at His courage but were afraid of the fate awaiting them in Jerusalem; although they were afraid, they still followed Him. Something we often don't think about is the courage of Jesus. It took a lot of bravery for Him to walk straight towards His fate at Calvary, *and* to walk *in front* of His disciples. He was not afraid to stand up for us. To be delivered to the Gentiles means that Jesus will be disrespected by His

Have you ever been put in a position where you had to stand up for what you believe in but don't know how to stand? We all have, and we will be in that position a lot more as we grow older and learn more about the world. There will be times at school and at work where someone will ask you about what you believe in, and you will need to be ready to give an answer. By reading God's Word and praying to Him for guidance, we will develop the same strength, courage, and bravery that Christ had when He stood up for us on the way to the Cross.

own people. Not to mention the shame of His suffering, we are reminded of His humiliation and suffering. The disciples rejoiced in identifying with Jesus and gladly suffered shame if they had to.

As David the Psalmist said, we need to be like the mighty ones and worship the Lord of beauty, and as we read in Joel's prophecy, we need to reject the wine of the world to rejoice in the life-giving wine, being the ultimate sacrifice of Christ our Lord. Also, as we read in Mark's Gospel, we need to follow Him to the Cross and trust Him regardless of the situation. So, how will you follow Him this week?

> *"Let me follow You wherever you go, even to Golgotha. It is not important for me to know where You will be leading me. The important thing is to follow You anywhere, even if You are taking me to the Golgotha. I will follow You even if there are persecutions and tribulations. If you lead me to the banks of the river, I will be there. Where You are taking me is inconsequential. I set neither limits, nor conditions. It just suffices to be with You."*
>
> *+ Pope Shenouda III +*

NINTH HOUR
STICK TO HIS WORD

Micah 2:3-10	Ps. 17:6	Mark 8:27-32

The prophecy from the book of Micah talks about that cruel day of judgement, and how the people did not receive God's Word. Does this sound familiar? The people of God, unfortunately, practised injustice, so God brought disaster upon them. Micah rebukes the pride among God's people and announces that the time of judgement is coming, and they will be brought low and will no longer walk arrogantly. Although they sinned against His Word, He still promised restoration to His people. When the prophets came to His people, they disregarded His Word. The key to preserving yourself in the midst of judgement is to stick tightly to His Word. When they rejected God's words, they were left poor, both materially and spiritually. In the last verse, Micah is exposing those false prophets, showing that they can never really give rest, therefore their words bring destruction instead of peace. With judgement looming on the horizon, there were false prophets who spoke of days of wine and drink, giving false comfort and hope to a deceived people.

The Psalm of this hour is very important when contrasted with the prophecy and upcoming Gospel. Psalm seventeen is a model of prayer – David does not ask for what he wants, rather explaining to God what is happening and waiting for His answer. *"I have called upon You, for You will hear me"* (Psalm 17:6). Can you feel the confidence David has in God? David was in the middle of a crisis when he wrote this, (like always(; but he had this confidence in God that He would hear his prayer whenever he called. Those who persevere in the ways of God will receive their daily dosage of grace and strength from Him, for He hears their cry. David prayed to the Lord and accepted His Word unlike the people in the prophecy of Micah who rejected it and wereeft with nothing. As I mentioned before, the key to preserving yourself in the midst of crisis is to stick tightly to Him and His Word.

Every day, whether we realise it or not, we are rejected by the world for following our Lord. But what do we do each time? We rise. No matter how tough it can become, we must remember that Christ went through the same rejection, and worse, and He still rose. We rise with our Lord like David did when he was in a crisis. We rise that we may walk with God in newness of life because He will hear our cry. Our Father, we killed Him, and we will kill Him again, and our world will kill Him. Yet He is still there. It is He who waits at the door of our hearts and is He who came through Christ. It was He who willingly went to the Cross, and it was our sins and rejection that took Him there.

As for the Gospel, it's true, we did just read the same passage from the Third Hour, but there's a different message this time. The people in the book of Micah rejected God, and this foreshadows those who Christ speaks of rejecting and killing Him: the elders and chief priests and scribes. There is a bit of a pattern going on here; first He was rejected, then He was accepted, now He is rejected again... by the same people! However, it is ironic because here Peter is declaring that Christ is indeed God but will later deny Him because he was scared, similar to the people that Micah warns who rejected God because they were scared of Him and His judgement.

ELEVENTH HOUR
A MUSTARD SEED

Micah 3:1-4	Ps. 18:17-18	Matt. 17:19-23

The further we are from Him and the less we know Him, the less we can do in His name because of our unbelief. The prophet Micah had great love for God and the souls of men, deep concern for His glory and their salvation and was against sin. The difficulties he met did not drive him away from his work. He relied on strength; not from himself, but he was full of power by the Spirit of the Lord. Those who act honestly may act boldly. And those who come to hear the word of God, must be willing to be told of their faults, and be thankful.

David felt that he was drowning when the strong hand of God picked him up out of many waters. Like a man in a flood, David knew that his enemies were too strong for him, but he had confidence that God would deliver him – God is among you. The strong hand of God not only plucked David out from the flood, but it also set him in a safe place. David was delighted as the Lord chose him, anointed him, and set His marvellous lovingkindness on him. How many times can you say that the Lord pulled you out of deep waters when you were drowning?

The use of "water" in this Psalm is also a metaphor for our faith, just like the mustard seed in the Gospel of Matthew. The disciples came to Jesus asking why they could not cast out the evil spirit. Christ responds with three things: the parable of the mustard seed, prayer and fasting, and a prophecy about His death, again.

The parable of the mustard seed in our Gospel is one which describes the humble beginnings of the Church that experiences an explosive rate of growth. The mustard seed is one the smallest seeds, but it produces a massive tree which grows to become a source of food, rest, and shelter. Like our Church when it first began, it was small, but now it has flourished into a beautiful and universal community. If faith as small as a mustard seed can do that, then believe that it can move mountains!

Another cool thing about mustard seeds is that they can grow in hot, dry, wet, and cold weather. The mustard seed is symbolic of faith, that it can grow in the most difficult of times – the seed never stops growing. We can go through extremely tough times, but we shouldn't let them stop us from growing and choosing to trust in a God that has a plan for each and every one of us. It is definitely easier said than done, but when we look at the characters in the Bible like Micah and David, we see that it is possible to get out of deep waters if we choose to let our faith move us to safety.

❧

Never underestimate yourself because you are stronger than you think! It can be very easy to look at other girls and see all of their success, but you need to remember that you are that girl as well! The best feature of a Christian girl is her strength, and no matter how small you may think you are, you are strong! You can do incredible things in this world. The Creator of this world knew what He was doing when He made you, you're in the palm of His hands, trust Him!

Holy Monday
Tree of Life

Holy Monday focuses on the story of Adam and Eve – their creation, sin, and removal from the Garden of Even. Once they sinned, they could not no longer remain in Eden because good and evil cannot coexist. It is through the passion of our Lord that we are able to eat of the Tree of Life, the Cross, which gives us the fruit of salvation and eternal life.

FIRST HOUR
THE FIG TREE

Gen. 1:1-2:3	Sir. 1:1-17	Ps. 72:18-19
	Mark 11:12-24	

As Adam and Eve covered their sin with the fig tree, Christ rebukes the fig tree to show that we can no longer cover our sins with a cloak of hypocrisy. As St. John Chrysostom said, *"The fig tree with its broad leaves represents the wide road. Also, it reminds us of the sin which Adam tried to cover with its leaves."* Adorn yourselves with truth so you will not experience the wrath of God, but His mercy. The Lord has made everything that is good; in His image and likeness, He created man and saw that it was good. Man has leaned towards sin, left God, saddened His heart, and hid with fig leaves. The Lord waited to see the fruit man would produce but did not. We cannot be hypocritical in our ways, but wise, as the Son of Sirach says in his prophecy; *"to fear the Lord is the beginning of wisdom; she is created with the faithful in the womb"* (Sirach 1:14). It is this tree of wisdom that was before all creation, the tree of life, the Cross, and its fruit is the Lord Himself.

The Psalm of this hour speaks of the wondrous and

glorious things the Lord has filled the earth with. He created all things and *"saw that it was good"* as it was according to His Divine plan. I want you all to know that our Creator has made everything in its time and in its season, and for every plan, there is a purpose, including you! If you ever find yourself in a situation where you question His plan, just look at yourself and admire what He has made. Everything takes time in order for it to be made well; time produces excellence. When God created you, He saw that you were good. He saw your heart and loved it from the moment He made you. God loves us for who we are.

On the Eve of Palm Sunday, our Lord went with His disciples outside the city. Along the way to Bethany, Christ was hungry; and He cursed a fig tree with many leaves but no fruit. This was a symbol of the Jewish nation, which had the outward appearance of fruits because they had followed the letter of the law.

As girls, we can be really concerned with our outer appearances, which is not a bad thing. But we need to give the same amount of attention and detail to the inside of our hearts because at the end of the day, that's the only thing God cares about! We can all sit behind a screen for hours editing a photo to make sure it's up to standard with our social media culture. We can even go to church every single Sunday to keep up our appearances as good Christian girls, but has our heart changed? Although we may look nice and pretty on the outside, we need to make sure our heart is just as beautiful.

However, they lacked fruit because they did not abide by the Spirit of the law and *"neglected the weightier things of the law"* (Matt. 23:23). The Lord did not curse the fig tree because it had no fruits, but because the leaves gave a false promise of bearing fruits. God rebukes a fruitless person. The Jewish nation boasted that they were a blessed people because of the Law, the temple, and religious rituals. However, they lacked faith, love, and holiness to accept Christ and obey His commandments.

The Church is reminding us that we should not think of this week as simply an outer appearance of worship without sowing the fruits of repentance, love, and meekness. Pray that you receive them, and you will have them. Have faith and God will grant you the desires of your heart. Be fruitful and repent to gain forgiveness. Think about how much Christ has suffered for you to save you.

THIRD HOUR
SIN AND PUNISHMENT

Is. 5:20-30	Jer. 9:12-19	Ps. 122:1-2
	Mark 11:11-19	

The prophecy of Isaiah is a description of the Assyrian army and its invasion of God's people. It gives a description that reveals the severity and aggression of the invasion of the human soul by the devil. At the same time, Isaiah rebukes loose believers. The wicked, for the sake of worldly benefit, would not linger until they realise their goal; while the children of God are not zealous enough to gain the fellowship of eternal glory. This prophecy describes how the people of God reacted to the Assyrian invasion. Despite the long distance hey walked for the reward, they did not get tired because of their strong desire for it; while believers can be careless in spiritual strife, under the pretence of exhaustion and weariness. Verses twenty eight to thirty are warnings that we, as a Church, must be ready for the day of the Lord. Ready your weapons to fight mightily until you realise your goal of salvation. Ready yourself for battle against the devil, with the spiritual weapons of faith, and *"let us gird our waist"* (Luke 12:35). The prophecy given by Jeremiah in this hour also paints an image of the destruction upon Jerusalem at the hands of its invaders.

The Psalm of this hour is simply an expression of the joy felt by those who love God and His sanctuary – also known as the Lord's entry into Jerusalem. The heart is drawn to the house of prayer; the soul is filled with peace at the knowledge of being able to worship God. When it says, *"let us go"*, it is an encouragement for us as readers to bring our fellow brethren to the house of the Lord. It can be easy to find something sinful in the world to "let it all out" on. While this can seem like an easy way out, it is much better to go to God's House and talk to Him. Take your friends to your Friend upstairs, He is waiting to talk to you too.

In the Gospel of St. Mark, the Lord was hungry. This does not imply that Christ was weak because His divinity never departed from His humanity; the Father and the Son are one. This has two meanings – He was not only hungry to feed His human body, but also His soul in knowing that there might be fruit He can reap from His people. When Christ saw only leaves and no fruit on the fig tree, He lost His appetite and then cursed the tree. Like Christ, we need to be hungry enough to fill ourselves with the fruit God has granted us. Our outer appearance to Him is nothing, all He cares is for the fruit we are to bear. I know I have said this in an earlier reading, but it is good to refresh your mind. The temple where Christ turned the tables in is our hearts, our minds, and lives. When we were baptised, Christ in His Spirit, came into us and became one in us. So, when He sees that you are filled with the things that are being sold in you, He comes in and flips everything upside down.

Like the people of God who were attacked by the Assyrian army, we need to prepare ourselves for what will come our way, and when we are prepared, we must go into the house of the Lord, as David tells us to. When we surrender ourselves to the Lord, He will begin to turn the tables in your life and take out what is evil and put in what is good. He will turn your *"den of thieves"* into a *"house of prayer."* He desires for you. Be hungry for Him just as He is hungry for you.

SIXTH HOUR
GOOD AND EVIL CANNOT CO-EXIST

Ex. 32:7-15	Wisd. 1:1-19	Ps. 122:4
	John 2:13-17	

The prophecy read from Exodus shows Israel asking for a god of their own making, a calf after God had delivered them from slavery in Egypt. How could the Israelites change the place of forgiveness into a place of sin, and a house of prayer into a den of thieves? What can they profit? You can imagine that God was mad about this, but Moses reminded God that these were His people and asked for their forgiveness instead of wrath. Moses also reminded God of His own promises. He did not want God to destroy His people according to His earlier promises of Abraham, Isaac, and Jacob. He has provided us with *that* mercy at the greatest cost to Himself, for Jesus was even more than a faithful servant unlike Abraham, Isaac, or Jacob. He was God's own Son, whom God gave on our behalf to save us.

Now, the reading from Wisdom is a bit random to some readers but trust me when I say it is relevant. This reading is a warning to the readers who neglect reading 'wisdom', being the Word. After reading this, I cannot help but think of the verse *"seek and you will find"* (Matthew 7:7). The first verse of the reading of Wisdom even says to *"seek him with sincerity of heart; because he is found."* How can it not stand out that this is God saying to come to Him?! He is always there waiting for you to come to Him because He never forces Himself onto anyone. He is found in *"foolish thoughts,"* in the *"inmost feelings,"* and even in the *"ungodly man."* The point of this reading is to show the readers that even if you are ungodly or unrighteous, God is found when you seek Him. Similar to Moses in the previous prophecy, we are to seek Him and ask for His mercy and forgiveness that we may be saved according to His promises.

The Psalm of this hour is a continuation of the previous hour. One of the main reasons David conquered Jerusalem was because it did not belong to a tribe under the Canaanites, so the tribes of the Lord were unable to come together in unity in the house of the Lord. The main purpose of these gatherings was to *"give thanks to the name of the Lord"*; to appreciate what He had done for them and what He would do for them in the future. This was an act of loyalty as the Lord commanded them to present themselves before Him. As Christians today, we should reflect this unity regardless of our diversity. David sought God, found Him, and shared Him as we ought to.

As for the Gospel, I know what you are thinking: "how many times do we need to read the same thing?!" Do not worry, this is the last time! I want us to focus on two overlooked verses in this Gospel, the first half of verse fifteen and verse seventeen. *"He made a whip of cords"* Christ made the whip He used to drive out all those He found selling in the temple. Creation requires intention, and His intention was salvation. This purposeful act was full of passion and was quick-minded because He stuck to His intention. After this, the disciples are reminded of Psalm 69:9, which refers to Christ. To be zealous means to be passionate, full of energy and devoted. Christ's passion for the purity of the temple is quite clear here. This says a lot about Christ's character and the powerful presence He had. However, this generated hatred from the surrounding religious leaders who would later *"eat Him up."*

So, Christ had made a whip of cords and drove everything sinful out from the temple. Let us not be like Israel and deprive ourselves of His help and support, seek Him in His temple and dwell in the house of the Lord forever! We cannot have evil and good in our hearts, we need to fill ourselves up with God and His love.

Ninth Hour
Knowledge of Good and Evil

Gen. 2:15-3:24	Is. 40:1-5	Prov. 1:1-19
Ps. 65:5	Matt. 21:23-27	

My first question: why would the reading of this hour be about a man being in union with a woman? In the marriage union, the husband and wife become *"one flesh,"* which St. Paul describes as a great mystery in the Church (Ephesians 5:32). This mystery is so great that the joining of the two is a sacrificial and devotional love because man is to leave his father and mother, with their blessing, and be joined in marriage. This mystery points to the greater mystery relevant to us: the marriage of Christ and His Bride, the Church. He left His Father and became Man to seek a Bride. He loved His Bride and gave Himself for her – does this sound familiar?

The next passage according to Isaiah is a prophecy about John the Baptist, who will be the voice proclaiming the coming of salvation through baptism into Christ our God (John 1:23). Isaiah repeats the word *"comfort"* twice, for He is talking about the Church of the New Testament and its categories: Jews and Gentiles. It is the Church of love that unifies and binds God to it, as a Groom and His Bride; and that binds the members coming from all nations, as one body and one head. Through this love, He addresses it saying, *"Speak comfort to Jerusalem,"* which literally translates to *"speak kindly to the heart of Jerusalem,"* an expression used in the Old Testament to address someone beloved. The Church here is the beloved Bride of Christ, whom He addresses with the language of love, understood only by the heart – the same language He spoke with, more openly and deeply through the Cross, to acquire humanity as His Bride. From the prophetical side, as the Bride looks at her crucified Groom, she finds that He completely paid her debt, not only for the sake of relieving her from it, but also to justify her by His blood, and to sanctify her, to enjoy the share in His glories. You are His Bride, He did this all because of His crazy love for you!

A lot of questions arise with this next reading, so I will keep it brief. The Fall of Adam brought a lot into the world; sin, hunger, pain, suffering, tragedy, death. Adam's disobedience cursed the ground and placed mankind under toil and labour until his end in death and decay in the grave. When Adam willingly disobeyed God's commandment, he fell from God's path of perfection and separated himself from the Source of Life. Christ, by His death and resurrection, conquered the devil and death, freeing mankind from the fear of death and making possible a more complete communion between God and humankind than was ever possible before.

Our final prophecy from Proverbs is simply an introduction to the Book. The word *"wisdom"* in Scripture means 'the ability to use knowledge right,' whereas *"instruction"* is to incorporate practicality; teaching, discipline, training. People may have the knowledge, but they lack wisdom and therefore may not use their knowledge correctly. This lack of wisdom is what led Adam to fall; he knew not to eat of the fruit but was not wise in his decision when he ate of it. We need to be careful when we make decisions, asking God for His wisdom and not our own. Wisdom is personified in Proverbs like a father and mother to His children, for He has deep love and affection for them. The Psalm here is a "wisdom psalm" and it matches the theme from Proverbs. It declares what we will receive when we stand in the courts of God – blessings on blessings.

The Gospel of this hour is a passage from our Lord when He speaks with the Pharisees. As man first fell through the tricks of the serpent, our Lord renewed man with His infinite wisdom. The high priests, scribes, and Pharisees challenged our Lord and His disciples with many theological debates. But our Lord explained the truth, in all wisdom and truth. The Pharisees were confused and were afraid of the Lord, so they refrained from answering Christ's questions, saying that they were not seeking the truth and were not worthy of recognizing it.

Eleventh Hour
Sold into Slavery

Is. 50:1-3	Sir. 1:20-30	Ps. 13:3-4
	John 8:51-59	

We were sold into slavery because of our sins, another warning of hypocrisy. The prophecy of Isaiah gives us a history of a certificate of divorce. When a Jew is divorcing his wife, even without reasonable cause, he used to give her a certificate of divorce before sending her out of his house. He could also sell her as a slave to his creditors and could sell his children as well. God did not do that to them, He is asking the Jewish nation who denied Him, and rejected His faith, about her certificate of divorce, in confirmation that He did not intend to divorce or dismiss her, but she divorced herself by her own will, and dismissed herself out of God's house, breaking the holy matrimony. Just as we were sold into slavery because of our sins, the Lord in this prophecy threatens His disloyal bride with the bill of divorce.

> *"God does not wish us to perish but wants us to act always like a bride rejoicing for her Groom, and not like a rebellious wife who deserts her home."*
>
> + St. John Chrysostom +

The Church makes it clear in this hour that to be able to live in Christ, as our Saviour teaches us, we should be aware of the leaven of the Pharisees, which is hypocrisy. The true physician of our souls knows the danger of hypocrisy and where the disease lies. He loves the publicans and the sinners whose healing He can foresee. Jesus has no pity for hypocrisy because it is the root of all diseases. By justifying the sinner of his own eyes, hypocrisy prevents a sinner from healing. This warning of hypocrisy is taken from the Wisdom of Sirach. Sirach tells us to continue in the fear of the Lord, in all wisdom and instruction.

The Psalm of this hour shows the psalmist asking the Lord to *"hear him"* and to save him. Like the psalmist, we should ask the Lord to save us from eternal death and ask for salvation. If we are free from slavery, shouldn't we not have to ask to be saved? We are human, we are weak, we fall into the trap of sin every day without even realising it. It could be as simple as talking about someone for the way they look or act. God doesn't want that for us, He doesn't want us to feel trapped, so He calls us to Him, every single moment of every day so that we remember that we don't have to feel this way because He has paid the price for our freedom.

The last Gospel of the day shows the continuing accusations of the Jews. The Lord declares that they neither know Him nor the Father. This carries through with the theme of the day concerning the fig tree. The Jews in their lack of faith and understanding of Christ as the Son of God bore bad fruits from a bad tree. The Homily of St. Shenouda is included to connect Adam and Eve's sin with hypocrisy. He speaks of living a life of holiness in a sinful world. It speaks of the judgement of others with the same standard as ours. The sin of judgment is the most important to focus on during this Holy Week. For its source is pride, the source of all sin. It is through humility that we begin our path to Paradise. We can be very easily caught up in our own pride sometimes, holding ourselves up so high that we don't realise how hypocritical or judgemental we can be. This is not the reason we are free; we are free from the slavery of sin that we may work our way up to God through acts of humility and service.

Tuesday Eve
The Judge

This evening, we focus on a different aspect of the end of days – preparation as a Church on her way to meet her Bridegroom. We must always remember to light our inner lamps with vigil, prayer, and repentance.

First Hour
The Narrow Gate

| Zech. 1:1-6 | Ps. 62:7 | Luke 13:23-20 |

Prepare yourself to meet your Bridegroom, beginning with repentance. The prophecy from Zechariah speaks of God's plea to repentance. When we look to God, we should *want* to turn to Him and repent. Sometimes, we can turn away from God and often feel like God has turned away from us, but that is certainly not the case. He has never fallen away from us. Hear Him when He says to you, *"Return to Me, and I will return to you"* (Zech. 1:3). In simple terms, this means that He will return to us that we may return to Him. Can anyone really succeed in escaping from God? He who delivers him that turns to Him, punishes him that turns away. You may have a Judge by escaping, but you do have a father by returning.

> *"If I do not seek You, O Lord, do not leave me lost, but search for me."*
>
> + Pope Shenouda +

Not only will He accept us, but He is our rock, salvation, honour, and refuge. We are not only *saved* by God, but we are also made glorious because we have been made just out of ungodliness. Where our salvation is, there our glory is; for what is our salvation but the glory to be revealed? We must constantly be reminded that the Lord is a refuge to whom we flee for shelter. By jumping back to this hour's prophecy, we are also to remember that we must return to Him because it will help us understand this hour's Gospel as well of entering through the narrow gate. To give a brief, but very important, rundown of why the gate is narrow, I would refer to St. Cyril of Alexandria, who explains it plain and simple:

> "The broad path means a pleasure-loving life, luxurious feasts, parties and banquets; and everything which is unpleasing to God... Those who enter by the narrow gate must withdraw from all these things in order to be with Christ and feast with Him."

Here is a scenario some readers might be familiar with: Passion Week comes along, and I say, "I'm going to give up all social media for the whole week and focus on my spiritual life! When Passion Week ends, I return to the same life with the same luxuries as if the week never happened. This is a reality and we have all been there! This hour's message teaches us that once we are willing to accept the call to repentance, as we do at the beginning of Passion Week, we must begin our struggle and travel along the narrow gate which leads to the Heavenly Kingdom. This requires us to continue spiritual sacrifices that we do for Passion Week all year 'round. Just as the Church reminds us of the knocking on the door of the wise and foolish virgins; those who entered the gate were only the holy, righteous and wise virgins. Run quickly before the door is shut, follow the way to the Cross!

THIRD HOUR
EMBRACE HIM

Mal. 1:1-9	Ps. 13:3-5	Luke 13:31-35

The prophecy from the book of Malachi shows God criticizing his people, and being very straight-forward about it as well: *"I have loved you says the Lord...If then I am the Father, where is My reverence?"* (Mal. 1:6). God wants sweet and real fruits from us, not the bad ones. Hypocrisy might get us praise from people but blessed are those whom God praises! It is God's desire to gather the fruits of His children since He is hungry for love. Who will offer these fruits to Him? Malachi makes mention of Esau: why? Well, Esau despised his brother, and God too. The brothers of Joseph also despised him and God. The Israelites despised Moses, and the sons of Eli despised the people, all the while despising God. Let us learn to not despise one another, lest we learn to despise God. Learn to honour each other [the lame and the sick] so that we may honour God and not be like the hypocrites God turns aside but the sweet fruit He desires.

How much longer will we forget Him? The Psalmist is asking God to enlighten his eyes. The eyes of the heart must be understood, that they may not be closed by the pleasures of sin. We need the light of God to shine upon us and give us His wisdom and knowledge lest we fall into spiritual death. It seems here that David felt that God was not listening; how often do we feel that? Yet, we should continue to cry out because God is honoured when we cry out to Him. After his prayer,

David comes to a moment of confidence and trust, which is why he begins to rejoice in the salvation of the Lord. Sometimes, it can feel like we are talking to a brick wall when we pray because we don't get an immediate answer. But when our prayers are answered, we are overcome with so much joy. Don't feel like God isn't listening to you, because He is, you just need to be confident and trust that He has an answer because He does; it is just coming when it's supposed to.

God is eager to embrace us and gather our fruits. In the Gospel, Jesus knew the destruction that would come upon Jerusalem, He knew that He was their salvation. The metaphor of the *hen* is often overlooked. When a hen sees that a beast is coming, she makes a big fuss to assemble her chicks so that she may protect them with her wings. Likewise, the Roman "eagle" is about to fall upon the Jewish empire, nothing can prevent this but running to God and embracing Him. Because the Jews would not "assemble" and come to Christ, the Roman eagle destroyed them. Likewise, we should run to God, He came to protect us, but we received Him in betrayal and hatred. But what is it that He came to protect us from? The *"fox,"*, otherwise known as Satan. We need to be aware that Satan can come as fox or a lion. We often just wait for a lion to come along to destroy us, but a fox lives among us and deceives us.

We must learn to be the sweet fruit God craves and open our eyes and embrace Him who was sent to protect and save us.

SIXTH HOUR
OBEY THE LORD

Hosea 4:15-5:7	Ps. 91:2-3	Luke 21:34-38

After Israel committed wickedness against her Bridegroom, the Lord rebuked the entire church in the book of Hosea, saying that He will instruct and correct us. At the time this prophecy was written, God's people were divided into two nations – Israel to the north, and Judah to the south. As for the cities of *"Gilgal"* and *"Beth Aven"* ('House of Deceit'), they were centres of idolatry (idol worship) in Israel. For a citizen from Judah to travel there meant that they shared in Israel's idolatry. This is a good message for us today, as when we get too close to sinful practices, they can often get rubbed off onto us. Arrogantly and stubbornly, Israel rebelled against God's word because of their pride. When God promised to leave the rebellious Israel, it meant that when it came time for them to repent, it was not considered genuine because they did not direct their actions toward turning back to God. We can be so set in our ways of rebelling that God can leave us to ourselves; *"He has withdrawn Himself from them"* (Hosea 5:6). Sometimes when we don't feel the presence of God in our lives, we can push Him away. However, every time we return to God, He is always compassionate and forgiving.

The Psalm describes the intensity of spiritual warfare that the Church fights against the devil. Success in this war is salvation, which comes through God and our hope in Him. His salvation is described as a *refuge* from the *hunters*. There are times when Satan can overwhelm us with worldly obsessions and passions, just as the Israelites were, and drive us away from the path to Christ. Our spiritual lives are protected by God's grace from the temptations of Satan.

*

How great is it that God Himself is our protector? He who has given us life has created a defence line for us, that we might be protected from every troublesome matter. Let us look at an example: at school or work, your coworkers or classmates might talk about you because of a bad haircut. Yes, you can feel upset by what is being said about you, but what you need to remember in a situation like this is that God sees your beauty and worth no matter what. This is what God's protection for us is like – He reminds you of His love when you might not feel it.

In the Gospel, The Lord teaches us not to fall into the sins of drunkenness and worry – or else we will receive the same judgement as Israel did in the prophecy of Hosea. The Lord, as our Teacher, taught early in the daytime in the temple to send a subtle yet important message. Christ is also telling us that excessive eating strains the heart and drains the power from the body. We must be strong and healthy so that we are ready for Christ when He comes to us. Christ was explaining the message that at all times of the day we should be ready with the fruits of repentance and love. A good example of us already doing this is every Sunday morning. We wake up early in the morning and all the people come to Him in the Church to hear Him. The best part about this? It's free! All we have to do is be diligent and obey

His teachings.

NINTH HOUR
"WOE TO YOU, HYPOCRITES!"

Hosea 10:12-11:2   Ps. 33:10-11   Luke 11:37-52

Continuing from the previous hour, God is telling Israel to soften their hardened hearts. God does this by building a picture of sowing and harvest – Israel has now sown the seed of sin and would soon reap the judgement of God. However, if they try to start sowing *righteousness*, they would then *"reap in mercy"* at the next harvest. If the ground, our hearts, are hard and stubborn and resist the seed, it must be broken up so it becomes fruitful. Sometimes when we hear the word of God, it can have little effect, because it falls onto the *fallow ground*, our hard hearts. Since the fallow ground is hard, it does not want to be broken up, and that is why we must seek the Lord. If we trust ourselves instead of God, then ruin will come upon us as it did for Israel. We must remind ourselves that although the harvest may *look* nice and pretty with leaves and branches, it does not mean that the seed which was sown is *fruitful*. This sounds familiar, doesn't it? Kind of like when Christ cursed the fig tree that looked beautiful but bore no fruit? We are now reminded that we must prepare our hearts and focus on the inner being and the seed we sow, that the fruits of repentance and love are brought forth.

The Psalm of this hour seems a bit out of place to some but allow me to explain. *"The Lord frustrates the counsel of the sinners"* of those who seek their own kingdoms, not the Heavenly Kingdom, those who seek earthly happiness and seek to rule. This takes us back to the prophecy – we must harden our hearts to the world and soften them to our God. The psalmist has praised God for His guiding hand as He moves along to the Gentile nations and softens their hearts, as we should allow Him. The word "counsel" in this instance means guidance, so when it says that *"the counsel of the Lord stands forever,"* it is because through all the tough times His people have gone through, God has never changed. Though the times are changing, the thing which remains constant in our lives is God, which is why His guidance will last forever. As for us, although we might change physically, spiritually we must remain constant and not be like the hypocrites which we will explore in the Gospel.

This hour is amazing – it is almost like the prophecy of this hour was written especially for this Gospel! Christ is rebuking the Pharisees about their concern for external matters only, which was the washing of their hands before dinner. It is not that Christ was being unhygienic for not washing His hands, He just didn't follow the extremely strict Jewish requirements of ceremonial washing. If only the Pharisees cared more about cleaning their hearts as they were did their hands, they would be more godly men. These Pharisees were also more careful to maintain the *appearance* of righteousness, *the outside of the cup*, but not the *inner* reality of it. Being good at all the outward things of Christianity does not necessarily mean you are a good Christian – sorry for the reality check! We can go to Church every Sunday, but unless our hearts are filled with love, then we are only fooling ourselves. It cannot be stressed enough that we need to care more about preparing our hearts and not our outward image. It does not matter how many likes you just got on your new profile picture, what matters is how much love you have for God, yourself, and others.

Eleventh Hour
Wait on the Lord

| Amos 5:6-14 | Ps. 122:4 | Mark 13:32-14:2 |

The theme of preparing our hearts continues through this hour. The prophecy of Amos speaks of the final days and the wickedness of man. When Israel was about to face judgement, the key to survival was to simply seek the Lord. However, if we are seeking places of disobedience, such as Bethel, we will not be able to seek the Lord. In the Old Testament, Bethel was a place of great spiritual heritage; it was the place where God met Jacob, but now they have turned it into a place of empty worship. Amos explains why God is worthy to be sought, and why He can deliver Israel from their judgement. He can do it because He is the God Almighty and is wise enough to make *"Pleiades and Orion"* (Amos 5:8), the star constellations. God is strong enough to save but is also strong enough to bring judgement. The Lord is with us as long as we simply seek good and not evil and transform our corrupt nature. Again, we must prepare our hearts for the Lord by prioritising what is good and seeking the Lord. It can be hard, putting God before your friends or even social media, but we need to remember that He always puts us first.

Another way to prepare our hearts is to go up and receive instruction from the Lord. Like Israel, the holy city goes up to the Lord to receive its commandments, so must we go to God and listen to His instruction. By going to the Lord, we continue to seek Him, as we discussed in the prophecy. We must not neglect what God has to say and we must give thanks for everything He says, particularly if it has anything to do with the final days. By continually seeking the Lord, we are preparing our hearts for His coming.

Pay close attention to this Gospel because we face the danger of being unprepared as *"that day and hour no one knows"* (Mark 13:32) draws near. A common question about this Gospel is "how could Jesus not know? If He is God, doesn't He know all things?" Jesus did not know the hour of the coming because He voluntarily, in submission to the Father, restricted His knowledge of this event. Yes, Christ is the Lord God, but He did not abuse His power to know everything because He was still human. Christ teaches us to *watch* because if you watch carefully for something, you won't be caught by surprise. The more we expect our Lord, the more we keep ourselves in readiness. Christ speaks to His followers about how they should live until He does return. He says that He is like a man going to a far country and leaves His servants with three things; His house, authority, and work. If we are to serve the Lord, we must serve His house, authority, work, service and Church that He has left for us. He also keeps a doorkeeper to watch because He may return at any time and does not want to find His servants sleeping! This Gospel continues to the next chapter as it speaks about the Passover. The time of Passover was significant because it was a time when the Messiah was expected to come. Since Passover remembered the time when God raised up a great deliverer and freed Israel from injustice, it was a time of great anticipation. The Romans were on guard and ready for anything. Every possible preparation was made for the Passover – this is the attitude we should have *daily*, as we look forward to the coming of our Lord. Seek the Lord, do good, and wait on Him.

Holy Tuesday
"Behold, the Bridegroom!"

Today we focus on the Lord as our Bridegroom, that we may have hearts that desire the Lord and be like the five wise virgins, who were prepared and ready for His coming.

FIRST HOUR
CALLED TO GOD

Ex. 19:1-9	Job 23:2-24:25	Hosea 4:1-8
Ps. 120:2, 6-7		John 8:21-29

The prophecies of this hour describe the difference between those who choose to follow in the way of the Lord and the rest of the world. As Christians, we must understand the special calling we have. In the prophecy of Exodus, God declared to the people of Israel that they were chosen with a special calling to be holy and obedient; He calls them a *"special treasure"* (Ex. 19:5) as He intended for them to be a part of His great plan. God's love and care are shown to the people of Israel as He tells them that He bore them on *eagle's wings*. The thing about eagles is that they do not carry their young in their claws like other birds; instead the young attach themselves to the back of their mother and are protected from the arrows of any hunters. The deliverance of the people of Israel was not so that they could follow the world, but so that they could be God's people. God protects us from the arrows of the world every day. He covers us with His arms and reminds us that we are safe because we are His precious children.

The virtue of obedience is seen in the reading of Job, as God softened his heart so that he remained fearful and in obedience to God. The story of Job is one that is applicable to everyone today because of the number of sufferings he went through. At one stage, Job felt separated from God; previously he found comfort in God, but his current sufferings led him to feel like He could not find Him. It was at this lowest point of Job's life that he cried to the Lord for help. Job's friends insisted that God was against him, but Job stuck by Him. Although we are weak, and we stumble, we are taught to persevere and reach a state where we will sin no more and not doubt our God – we should stubbornly cling to Him. The book of Hosea brings together these three prophecies as it links back to the theme of the Bridesmaids and awaiting our Lord and being ready, as Hosea says, *"you shall stumble in the day"* (Hosea 4:5). It is bad enough that we stumble in the night when we are not ready, which is at least understandable. But when God's people cast off the knowledge and guidance of God, they shall stumble even in the day time.

The Psalm shows David recording his experience of when his friends deceived him and falsely accused him without cause. The people that David dwelt with not only hated him, but hated peace, and proclaimed war against it. Such was Christ's enemies: for His love, they were His enemies, and for His good words and works, they stoned Him. If we meet with such enemies, we must not think it strange, nor love peace less so that we don't seek it in vain. Likewise, the Jews hated and crucified Christ *without cause* because of the *deceitful tongue* with which Judas betrayed our Lord. We have deceitful tongues and betray our friends and God. We need to watch what we say or we will not have peace.

Christ continues talking to the disciples about His death to ensure they remain faithful and hopeful when the Jews lifted up the Son of Man on the Cross – if we follow Jesus on earth, we will follow Him to Heaven. We are reminded in this hour that we must choose to follow Christ because, like the eagle's wings, we are lifted on the Cross with Him; and like Job, we cling to God, and like David, we seek Him for peace.

THIRD HOUR
WE ARE TESTED

Deut. 8:11-20	Sir. 2:1-9	Job 27:1-28:2
1 King 19:9-14	Ps. 119:154-155	Matt. 23:37-24:2

The prophecies of this hour remind us to remain with God and not forget Him when we are tested. Often, when life is going well, we can easily forget the Lord and His work in our lives. We often think highly of our own hard work and efforts, yet we must see that it is God who has given us our bodies and our talents. Because it is all God's work, we have no right to use our material blessings to fulfil selfish purposes but rather use our gifts to glorify God. In the prophecy from the book of Deuteronomy, Moses warned the people of Israel against the sins of disobedience and pride. Pride is the greatest danger in the Christian life because it was pride brought Satan down. Yes, if you have accomplished something you should be happy. However, don't forget that it was God who pulled you through! The prophecy of Sirach reminds us to remain with God and to prepare for trials and tribulations, especially in service. Sirach uses the example of gold to describe the person who goes through trials. Gold is tested in the fire so that it becomes pure, like us, when we are tested and *cling to Him*, we will become like gold. Sirach warns us not to stray from God, but rather to hope for good things and to trust in Him.

The prophecy from the book of 1 Kings continues the theme of remaining steadfast in tribulation. This prophecy shows Elijah talking to God, and he mentions how *"zealous"* [passionate] and faithful he has been to God. For Elijah, and many servants since his time, it seemed unfair that a servant of God should be made to suffer. It makes sense at first glance – "I serve God, I'm faithful, but look at all the things that I'm going through." Elijah even says that he feels alone; how many times have we felt like that? As we continue through this prophecy, we see God revealing Himself to Elijah. God wasn't in the wind, nor the earthquake, nor the fire, but He was a *"still small voice."* Whenever we go through trials, we always look for God in our situations, and sometimes we can't find Him among all the noise, but when we sit down in front of Him and clear our minds to talk to Him, He will talk to us, ever so gently.

The psalm of this hour is a prayer by David and is a plea for justice in the middle of tribulations. This psalm reminds us that David's life was not easy, even though he was a king. David looked for help and salvation in the middle of his hurt because he knew that he needed God to redeem and save him. God is a source of revival; if we read His word and chase after God with our whole heart, we will be renewed! We are constantly being tested with trivial things; whether we should put reading our Bible before watching a new TV series or hanging out with friends before praying. It is not always easy to make these decisions, but when we look to God as a source of life, we will have a proper balance in our lives.

So, suffering; I think we know all too well who suffered the most in history, right? This reading from the Gospel of Matthew shows that just as Christ suffered, so must we. We read in this hour that Jesus wept over Jerusalem because He wanted to protect the people, like a hen gathers her chicks under her wings, from the judgement they would receive when they reject Him. This cry is a way for us to see that Jesus did not hate the men that rebuked Him. If anything, His heart was sad for them.

SIXTH HOUR
JUDGEMENT

Ezek. 21:3-13	Sir. 4:20-5:2	Is. 1:1-9
Ps. 18:48	John 8:12-20	

During this hour, we are reminded of the Lord's judgement, which Ezekiel describes as a *sword*; cutting off the wicked and setting aside the righteous. This sword is a testing sword, coming to cut off evil and sin; therefore, if someone turns from his evil, he will be saved, which is something we will understand more in this hour's Gospel. This prophecy according to Ezekiel reads dramatically and scary, but we should remember that this sword is sharpened for the wicked, not for the chosen children of God. We must remember our special calling as Christians; just as God told Moses that the people of Israel were chosen, so are we! In the reading of Sirach, we continue to see a message of turning from evil and not to be ashamed of confessing your sins. We must fight to the death for truth and have the determination to become righteous through the narrow road for the sake of our eternal life. We see this fight in the prophecy of Isaiah, where instead of fighting for the truth, the Israelites rebel against God and are no longer His people. Something that we must remember about Christ is that even when the Pharisees mistreated and persecuted Him, He still wept for them and never returned the same treatment, even though He had the power to do so. Even up until the point of His death, He felt sorry for them. Whenever we rebel against God and turn away from His judgement, we must constantly remember that He will continue to wait for us because we are His chosen children, His holy bride.

When we sin, we must remember that God does not hate us; He is sorry for us because He knows that sin and rebellion can ruin our lives, just as He prophesied the destruction of Jerusalem. We are the Jerusalem that Christ wept over, that He suffered for, it only makes sense for us to cling to Him when we suffer!

The Psalm was written by David when he felt that he was drowning under the strong hand of his enemy. While David knew that his enemies were too strong for him, he knew that God would not only deliver him but set him in a safe place. St. Augustine explains the verses in this Psalm as the prophecy of the Jews who revolted against Christ and cried out *"Crucify Him, crucify Him!"* To this, Christ says, "From the Jews that rise up against Me in My passion, You will exalt Me in My resurrection." In the same way, God will deliver Christ from death and the evil that attempts to rule over Him. Sometimes, the evil materialistic things of this world will want to take over us, but we need to look up to God and remind ourselves that He alone is the only One who can save us.

As the prophecy from Isaiah explains that Israel did not know God, so Christ explains that the *same* nation does not know the Father. Therefore there will be a judgement which separates the sons of Light and those of darkness. The *sword* we read about in Ezekiel separating the light from the dark is Christ in this Gospel, the true Light of the world. In this hour's Gospel reading, we are again reminded of God's judgement. Christ says, *"I judge no man... yet if I judge My judgement is true"* (John 8:16). If Christ had come to judge us, He would have condemned us and placed us with the wicked, but instead He came to save us according to the Father's love and mercy. But why does Christ go on a tangent and begin talking about the Father? It was because this reading was directly related to the prophecy of Isaiah for the children of Israel in both the Old and New Testament. They did not know the Father and did not recognise Christ as the Son of God. This points to the fact that the Father will come to judge, not Christ, as His time had not yet come for neither His crucifixion or judgement.

The readings of this hour show that the Kingdom is no longer for a specifically chosen nation or people – the Lord opens paradise to all people who have kept the covenant. God loves everyone, so He is *for* everyone. We can sometimes be quick to judge people and whether they are good enough or worthy. We need to be careful of this because we can quickly turn into hypocrites. We need to look at ourselves and our covenant with God and not other people. God's love is not limited because He looks at the heart and so should we.

NINTH HOUR
JUDGEMENT OF THE WICKED

Gen. 6:5-9:6	Prov. 9:1-11	Is. 40:9-31
Dan. 7:9-15	Prov. 8:1-12	Ps. 25:1-3
	Matt. 24:3-35	

During this hour, we focus on preparing ourselves for the Second Coming of Christ through repentance and the Sacraments. The prophecies of this hour represent different visions of God that were seen in the Old Testament. In Genesis, we read about the corruption of man and the righteousness of Noah's family, as well as the prophecy of the Second Coming through the Great Flood. We see the destruction of the earth in this passage due to sin. Between verses 5 and 13, the word *"earth"* is repeated 7 times to demonstrate how man became corrupted through the focus of worldly and material things. After the flood, Noah builds an altar to symbolise the Sacraments and thanksgiving. The flood was a symbol of baptism, but the offering of thanksgiving on the altar was a symbol of the Liturgy. We should also note that the ark itself symbolises

❈

While we remind ourselves of our unavoidable judgement, we must also remember that we are children of Light, not darkness and that we are chosen to be placed in a safe house with God because we are His bride and He is our beloved Bridegroom. Being His Bride means that, as a wife does to her husband, we go to Him for safety, we trust Him to provide for us because His duty is to take care of us, even unto death.

repentance. The eight people in the ark that were saved symbolised the Day of Resurrection and of the Second Coming. As we were washed with the waters of Baptism, we are cleansed once again with the sacrament of Repentance and Confession.

We read in Proverbs about the House of Wisdom, representing the Incarnation and Crucifixion of Christ. The Lord offers us salvation and the sacraments of His Church; *"Come, eat of my bread and drink of the wine I have mixed"* (Proverbs 9:5). This prophesies the Lord's water mingling with wine, as it will occur in the Lord's passion.

The prophecies according to Isaiah and Daniel explain two visions of the Second Coming, where both prophets see God sitting on His throne arrayed in majesty. Isaiah describes the grim fate of unbelievers – those who lack faith in God – while Daniel's prophecy is linked directly to the upcoming Gospel, *"the abomination of desolation"* and the coming of Christ to establish His kingdom in our hearts. The thrones in verse 9 refer in Hebrew to the thrones of kings that were removed so that the King of kings alone will judge. This theme will be mentioned again in the Eleventh hour concerning the throne of God. The *"open books"* in verse 10 refer to the books that contained people's sins. We should remember that we are the ones who write these books which will judge us on the Last Day, therefore being aware of every deed, whether good or evil, calling ourselves to repentance.

The Psalm of this hour shows David's desire towards God and his dependence on Him. By trusting ourselves, we were brought to the weakness of the flesh, we feared death from the smallest thing, we were ashamed of our pride, but now we put our trust in Him and should not be ashamed because He has come to save us.

The Gospel tells us that *"before the flood, the sons of men used to eat, drink, and multiply until the day Noah entered the ark as ordered by God"* (Matt. 24:38). They did not know about the flood by which everything would be destroyed. In the same way, in His Second Coming, all will be taken by surprise. In the same way, eight people were spared by the flood, we must remember Christ's words, *"For many are called, but few are chosen"* (Matt. 22:14). God gave us a complete sign of His Second Coming, for He speaks of the days against Christ. He calls it an *abomination* for men who come against God and seek honour for themselves. He calls it an *"abomination of desolation* [misery]*"* because although there will be wars and killings, it will not be the end. The Lord is coming, but when He comes, do not be deceived by false prophets, and look to the Heavens from which He will return for us.

"The Lord calls His body a carcass by reason of death…
but He calls us eagles, implying that he who draws near
to this Body must be on high and have nothing common
with the earth, nor wind himself downwards and creep
along; but must ever be soaring heavenwards, and look
on the Sun of Righteousness."

+ St. John Chrysostom +

ELEVENTH HOUR
BEFORE HIS THRONE

Is. 30:25-30	Prov. 6:20-7:4
Ps. 45:6, 41:1	Matt. 25:14-26:2

In this hour, we add "My Good Saviour" to our Paschal Praise of *Thok te ti gom*, "Thine is the Power." The Church wants us to realise that our Lord Jesus has specified the time of His passion and crucifixion as we read the Gospel – *"after two days is the feast of the Passover and the Son of Man shall be betrayed to be crucified"* (Matt. 26:2). It is during this hour the Church wishes to prepare us to view Christ as our Good Lord, our Bridegroom, from whom all good things come.

Isaiah explains that we must be prepared for our Lord's Second Coming as He will come *"burning with His anger, and in thick rising smoke."* He describes those who will deny Christ on the last day as spiritually dead, falling like towers. At the time, it was fitting for the Jewish to be leaders, towers for the world, to behold the kingdom of God and preach it. Instead, they became opponents of the Truth, so they fell. The ending of this prophecy paints a picture of the destruction of Assyria, describing how the *topeth*, the pit of fire, where the trash was burnt outside Jerusalem, was prepared and made ready for the king to burn with the wrath of the Lord. Proverbs explain the need to keep the commandments of our Lord; there is an emphasis here on adultery so that we do not forget who our first true love is.

The throne of God is a symbol of the judgement of the Second Coming. The Church has a special hymn for this Psalm, 'Pekethronos' (Πεκⲑⲣⲟⲛⲟⲥ, 'Your Throne'), as when we chant it, we are reminded of His righteous judgement. We will be chanting this Psalm again on the twelfth hour on Good Friday, during which the throne symbolises the Cross of our Lord. The Psalm and Gospel of this hour illustrate God sitting in His glory to judge and reward each one according to their deeds. Psalm 44 exclaims, *"Your throne, O God..."* with the Gospel saying something similar, *"...on the throne of Your glory."* The *"sceptre of righteousness"* is that which directs mankind from crookedness to righteousness.

The Psalm and Gospel of this hour work perfectly together as they illustrate God sitting on His throne to judge each one according to his acts, as we see in the Parable of the Talents. In preparing to leave this world, Christ is telling His disciples to continue His work and see to it that they and others attain salvation. In order to achieve this, Christ gives them talents, each according to his own strength. The lazy servant was cast into darkness, outside communion with God and His light. To avoid this, one must increase their talents. No matter how dark the clouds get in our lives, we must always look to the everlasting throne of God and remain faithful until the end of our earthly journey. This means to be faithful in not only in word but also in deed! We should learn to be merciful and loving to others before the day of Judgement and look to feed, take in, clothe, and visit the strangers, because what we do unto them, we have done to Him (Matt. 25:40).

Love the stranger just as much as you love your friends. When your friends ask you for help, you drop everything for them, right? Do the same for the stranger! Show your love through services through the Church, helping the homeless and visiting the sick.

Wednesday Eve
The Wedding Feast

The theme of this evening is our marriage with the Bridegroom, our union with God. The Church is preparing herself for eternal life with Him.

FIRST HOUR
THE WEDDING GARMENT

| Ezek. 22:23-29 | Ezek. 22:17-22 |
| Ps. 59:16-17 | Matt. 22:1-14 |

The focus of this hour is how we as the Church should wear the garment of purity and righteousness needed for our wedding day, the Day of Judgement. In the prophecy of Ezekiel, the Lord speaks as a coppersmith seeking to purify different types of metal in the furnace. He explains how He could not purify the house of Israel and must throw them in the midst of the fire and melt them. Now, don't get scared by this, there is a deeper meaning here! The Church fathers explain how each type of metal represents our struggles and outcomes. Let us take a look at some of these metals:

When *bronze* is struck, it becomes stronger than all other metals. Therefore, whoever breaks down when in the furnace, or struck by any kind of struggle, is likely to come out stronger than they ever were. But *tin*, when it is put in a mineral called ore, can make the metal appear to be silver when it is not. This metal is refined a lot so that something precious can be extracted. Likewise, we must always call ourselves to repentance so that we can be made pure like silver. *Iron*, when put into the furnace, symbolises the person who does not refine themselves and does not eliminate their sinfulness in their struggles. Finally, *lead* is the heaviest of the metals, so when it is placed in the furnace it does not find it a struggle. Likewise, we should not fall under the temptations of this world and rise above our tribulations, remaining strong. Just as the metal must be purified and cannot contain impure material, so too the soul must be as pure or else it will not celebrate the wedding feast in the kingdom of Heaven.

In this Psalm, we find David praising God, seeing that in the day of his tribulation he turns to God. How many times have we gone through a tough struggle and have found ourselves turning to God as a last resort? God brings His people into tribulations that they may see His power and mercy in protecting and sheltering them, seeing the chance to praise Him. But why would we praise Him in a struggle? Because we still depend on Him and have confidence in Him. Because we know it is His duty to keep us safe and to support us.

In the Gospel, we read the Parable of the Wedding Garment and find Christ comparing Heaven to a wedding banquet a king prepared for his son. Many people were invited, but when the time for the banquet had come, those who were invited *refused* to come and made up excuses. In fact, the king's servants who were sent to spread the invitation were mistreated and even killed! The king was so furious that he sent an army to avenge the death of his servants, as well as invitations to anyone he could find so that the wedding banquet was full. But he noticed a man not wearing a wedding garment, so he cast him out.

The king here is God the Father, and his son is Jesus Christ. Israel held the invitation to the Kingdom, but when the time came for the Kingdom to appear, they refused to believe it. Many prophets had been killed spreading this message. The king's vengeance on the death of his servants can be interpreted as a prophecy of Jerusalem's destruction by the Romans. This is not to say that God looks for revenge, but that He is patient and will not tolerate wickedness forever. His judgement will come to those who reject His offer of salvation, being His Son. The wedding invitation is offered to anyone and everyone, strangers both good and bad. The message of the Gospel is that Heaven is for everyone who accepts Christ and wears the wedding garment. The wedding garment is a symbol of the righteous life which is united fully with the Lord. Judas was this man without the heavenly garment because he not only denied salvation but also betrayed our Lord.

We are like metals that must be purified by the coppersmith; we must be pure enough to wear the wedding garment or we will be cast out of Heaven.

THIRD HOUR
THE BRIDE'S OIL

Amos 5:18-27	Ps. 65:4-5	Matt. 24:36-51

We must be ready for the true wedding, and cannot be eating, drinking, and given in marriage to the world and sin. The Lord wears the house of Israel as a sash that clings to Him, a symbol of our union and fellowship with Him and the heavenly life He prepares for us. One of the main themes of Passion Week is readiness and watchfulness. This is likened to the oil of the bride that will keep her awake and prepare her to meet the Bridegroom.

In the prophecy of Amos, we read of those who are celebrating a feast at an inappropriate time. God will reject their offerings and sacrifices because they were not paying attention and were distracted by sin and wickedness. The prophecy talks of the Last Day as someone fleeing from a lion but is then faced with a bear, who would be ready for that? Do these people know what death really is, do they not know that it will be dark with no light? When God makes a day dark, the world cannot make it light. It would be crazy not to think about the day of the Lord because, as scary as it sounds, there is no way to escape it. We need to chase after God, we need to seek and prepare ourselves for Him. We need to look forward to His coming and not fear it, because we have hope of being with Him in the Heavenly kingdom. The Psalm teaches us to be righteous and accept Him as our righteousness. Those who come into communion with God shall find true happiness and satisfaction because they are blessed. To come into communion with God is to approach and talk to Him as our one true love. God's temple is His House, where He dwells with an abundance of goodness, and there is enough for everyone all the time, free of charge.

Like the prophecy, the Gospel compares those who are celebrating by eating, drinking, and sinning with the ready, watchful, and righteous servant of God. This passage begins our focus on the parable of the ten virgins, which we will go through in the sixth hour. This parable has a unique role in the Church as it not only prepares for Pascha but is used in the Church as a daily reminder in the gospel of the First Watch of the Midnight Hour. Christ is telling us here that the hour of which He will return is unknown by man, even by the angels! This knowledge is reserved for the Father only. Christ says that His return will be like what the world was like in the days of Noah, where we centred our lives around worldly and sinful things. We should also remember here that those in the days of Noah were warned of the flood, and judgement eventually came. Those who ignored the warnings were not ready, and so it came unexpectedly.

Christ is really trying to emphasise to us in this Gospel that He will come at any given moment without warning. He even uses the parable of the two servants to drill this point. Until Christ returns, we must be like the faithful servant and take care of his master's business while he is away. We must minister to the Church and do the Lord's service until He comes back. Jesus also promised that we will be rewarded for this. We must not have the attitude of the evil servants and sin in the way they did; they did not do as their master told them, they mistreated their fellow servants, and they gave themselves into the pleasures of the world instead of serving their master.

The emphasis on constant readiness is a challenge for us, we can appear to be unprepared in the same way as the evil servants. Upon His return, we must follow the Lord's commandments and teachings, we must treat each other with love and respect, and we must not give in to worldly pleasures and desires because the Kingdom of Heaven is much better. Don't lose yourself to this world, give yourself to Christ.

Sixth Hour
Coming of the Bridegroom

Jer. 16:9-14	Ps. 102:1-2	Matt. 25:1-13

As we introduced the readiness of the faithful servant in the third hour, we continue this theme in this hour as we look deeper at the coming of our Bridegroom. This hour reminds us to have the oil of the Holy Spirit and the Sacraments so that we can enter the marriage, the Kingdom of Heaven. If we lack this oil, the door of salvation will be shut before us.

In the prophecy of Jeremiah, we read about how our Bridegroom clothes Himself with *us* as a sash that clings to Him. The sash the Lord wears is a symbol of His people, for He wishes to completely unite with us out of His love. If we are the clothes of Christ, we clothe His nakedness with our faith. The Lord would like for us to shine with Him, bright and holy. The two parables of the buried sash and the bottle filled with wine are related to each other and can be explained through this quote:

> "The first [the buried sash] refers to pride, the destroyer of man; and the second [the bottle filled with wine] refers to the drunkenness with sin and the lack of repentance... He probably used the two parables to refer to the denial of the soul, of the work of the Lord Christ, and its denial of His Holy Spirit."
>
> + Fr. Tadros Malaty +

The Psalm is like a bride's cry to her Bridegroom, as the Shulamite woman cried to her bridegroom in the Song of Solomon because of how much she loved him. This is our cry during the Pascha Week, to be united with our Beloved for the forgiveness of our sins and the salvation of our souls.

So, in the third hour, we briefly introduced readiness for the coming of the Lord. This theme is now continued in this hour's Gospel as we read the parable of the ten virgins. We read this gospel to refer to the coming of the Bridegroom and the suffering of the 5 foolish virgins. In this hour, we focus on His arrival and the rejection of the foolish virgins. Let us take a quick look at the historical setting of this parable as it describes a first-century Jewish wedding.

Normally, the bridegroom with his close friends would go to the bride's home for a small ceremony and procession through the streets, at night, and then return to his house. The ten virgins would have been the bridesmaids, and they expect to meet the groom as he comes from the bride's house. Each person in the procession was expected to carry their own lamps. If they didn't have one, they were assumed to be a party crasher. Now, the virgins didn't know when the groom would arrive at the bride's house, so they had to have a lamp-lit at all times to be ready for him, meaning they needed to have extra oil just in case their lamps burnt out. See where this is going?

In the parable, the five virgins who had extra oil represent those who are looking with eagerness for the coming of Christ. They have faith and determination to be ready at any given time. The other five virgins without the extra oil represent false believers who enjoy the things of the world without true love for Christ. They are more excited about the after-party than actually seeing the bridegroom. Their hope is that their relationship with the true believers, those who had extra oil, will bring them to the kingdom at the end; *"give us some of your oil."*

Prayer

How faithful have I been to You as a Bride?

Am I loving, honest, and caring as You have taught me?

Has my heart become cold for You,

My oil, vanished as the foolish virgins?

My compassionate Redeemer,

Allow me just a few moments to collect my oil.

Do not shut the door of salvation in my face.

Save me from my laziness, carelessness, and recklessness.

One person's faith cannot save another.

May we not be found to be looking for more oil when Christ returns. Take the time now to fill your lamp with oil and take extra. Keep waiting and watch with joy and anticipation!

NINTH HOUR
FOOLISH VIRGINS REJECTED

Hosea 9:14-10:2	Ps. 22:20-21	Matt. 23:29-36

This hour is like an introduction to the evil that is about to take place at the hands of the chief priests through their dealings with Christ. God remembers the days when Israel was faithful and fruitful to Him. In the previous verses of this same chapter (Hosea 9), it is written that Israel was so faithful and special that they were likened to grapes that grew in the wilderness, something unexpected. Hosea was a prophet that prayed for mercy, knowing of the judgement of the Lord. Israel had disgraced God's house and disobeyed Him by worshipping idols. Even when God blessed Israel with material abundances, like land, they spent it on themselves and in ungodly ways; *"he brings forth fruit for himself"* (Hose 10:1). Ephraim had become divided, God broke down their altars and ruined their sacred pillars, meaning He will come to judge them for their evil deeds. This passage is a symbol of the condemnation of the wicked. We discuss this prophecy again in the first hour of Holy Wednesday.

The Psalm shows David crying out to God to save him from his enemies. This was the cry of the prophet who asked for his soul to be saved from the sword, the lion, and other beasts. This symbolises the Jews who were persecuting the prophets. It is more than a coincidence that this Gospel and Psalm are read on the commemoration of the 40 saints of Sebaste (February 23rd), which usually falls in the middle of the week. These saints were brutally killed as the prophets were by the Jews. In this Gospel, Christ even speaks of the righteous prophets and martyrs of the Old Testament, namely Abel the son of Berechiah (2 Chronicles 24).

This hour's Gospel provides comfort to those mourning the righteous and demonstrates that the Just Judge will give each one according to his deeds. The same condemnation the Jews faced for killing their prophets, will be faced by the Jews who plotted to kill the Lord. It is interesting, the scribes and Pharisees rejected living prophets but respected the dead ones. This really does back up what Christ was saying, *"you are witnesses against yourselves that you are sons of those who murdered the prophets"* (Matt. 23:31). Christ even goes to the extent of calling them *"serpents, brood of vipers!"* (Matt. 23:33). This phrase basically translates to the idea that they are like the family of the devil. These religious leaders held great pride in their heritage, thinking they were the great sons of Abraham when they were really like sons of the devil. These men were the furthest away from God and needed to be warned of the coming judgement. He did not come to judge them and all He wanted was their repentance, which explains why it seems like He was really fed up with them!

This hour really drills into us that we should not be foolish, that we should not reject Christ and should persevere in times of struggle. Look to the martyrs for support, pray that we may put Christ first and not fall into the deceitful hands of this sinful world.

ELEVENTH HOUR
THE WISE BRIDE

Wisd. 7:24-30	Ps. 57:1	John 11:55-57

We continue to focus on the wisdom of the virgins and compare this with the foolishness of the Jews. We read from the Wisdom of Solomon to understand the qualities of wisdom, and how it is the *power of God*, and the reflection of His image and goodness. Verses 25 and 26 describe the wisdom of God; powerful, glorious, bright, good. Activity: swap the words 'wisdom' and 'she' with 'He/Him.'

"...*He* is a reflection of eternal light, a spotless image of the working of God, and an image of His goodness... *He* renews all things...for *He* is more beautiful than the sun...compared with the light *He* is found to be superior...but against *Him* evil does not prevail."

Sounds interesting right? Here we see the image of Christ presented to us, describing Him in all His greatness! But what is this "evil" in the final verse? What if we were to swap 'evil' with 'the Jewish rulers' or 'the Pharisees'? Nothing can *ever* prevail [triumph] against Christ because He is the image of God!

The Psalm is read during the sixth hour of the Agpeya [Book of Prayers] as it speaks directly of the Cross and the Passion of Christ. When David wrote this Psalm, he was surrounded by enemies, so he looked up to God with a prayer. He went to the Lord and declared his confidence in Him. *"In the shadow of Your wings I will make my refuge"* – this is closely related to the prophecy as Christ is about to be surrounded by His enemies, yet this evil will not prevail against Him because of his confidence in the Father. Like Christ, David was confident his troubles would end, in due time. Our Lord comforted Himself with this in His own sufferings – how often do we do the same?

In the Gospel, the Jews are preparing to kill the Lord – this helps to prepare us for Judas' betrayal. According to their tradition, the Jews went up to the mountain to purify themselves with the water of purification to prepare for the Passover. This teaches us to renew our repentance. When the Jews did not see Christ at this event, they wondered among themselves if He would come. When we expect to meet God, we must prepare ourselves. While hypocrites and worldly people pursue their own plans, Jesus orders all things for His glory and salvation of His people. As the prophecy and Psalm teach us, we need to look to the wisdom and refuge of God to not only be safe but to also prepare ourselves for His glorious coming!

Holy Wednesday
Kisses of Love & Betrayal

This day depicts two kinds of love – sacrificial love as performed by Mary of Bethany, and a betrayal of love by Judas. "With silver, you have sold Christ to the Jews, who had broken the law. But those contrary to the law they took Christ. They nailed Him on the Cross... Judas, who has broken the law."

From tonight, Thursday Eve, until the end of the Liturgy on Bright Saturday, kisses and greeting are not allowed by the Church. This is in rememberance of the betrayal of Christ by Judas with a kiss. Some Churches refer to this day as "Spy Wednesday" because it was the day of the great betrayal.

Today is a rollercoaster of a journey, as we will go through the stages of spiritual life. We will begin our journey in Ephraim, a place rich with fruit, yet near the wilderness. Those who seek the Lord in Ephraim will find fruit and satisfaction for their souls and bodies. However, those who do not go to Ephraim will find themselves in Etham, a symbol of the evil man that relies on his own strength, virtue, and efforts. He will end up like Judas, betraying his Master. So, to obtain this fruit, we must go to Bethany, to pour our hearts at the feet of our Lord in the form of rich oil. And then finally, we will go to carry our Cross in Jerusalem.

FIRST HOUR
"EPHRAIM"

Ex. 17:1-7	Prov. 3:5-14	Hosea 5:13-6:3
Sir. 1:14-4:30	Ps. 51:4-33:10	John 11:46-57

In the prophecy of Hosea, the Israelites complain that there is no water to drink after they passed from the Wilderness of Sin to camp in Rephidim. After we see their lack of faith, the remaining prophecies remind us of how faithful God was to them in their escape from Egypt. We can interpret their journey as that of a believer from the land of slavery to freedom as children of God. We travel from the land of Sin, temptation, to the land of Rephidim, the land of wisdom. In Hosea, we also see that although the land of Ephraim was fruitful, its joyful harvest was going to end and will not bear any more fruit under God's judgement. This prophecy also speaks of the Lord's resurrection and our resurrection with Him; *"After two days He will revive us; on the third day He will raise us up"* (Hosea 6:2).

The rock that Moses struck is a symbol of Christ, with the water coming out of it representing the Holy Spirit poured out onto all of us. The children of Israel tempted the Lord, saying *"Is the Lord among us or not?"* We leave room for sin when we begin asking if God is among us and doubting His presence. The prophecy from Proverbs confirms this by encouraging us to trust God, to honour Him and not question Him. The land of Israel was destined for fruitfulness and blessing, but it was turned desolate when it rejected and plotted Christ's death. This prophecy also introduces the soon to come betrayal of Christ by Judas: *"For the merchandise of wisdom is better than the merchandise of silver and the gain of gold"* (Proverbs 3:14). Judas should have reflected on this piece of wisdom when he sold out Jesus. We too should recall these words when tempted to betray or reject Jesus, as the prophecy of Sirach encourages us; *"keep the commandments…do not disobey the fear of the Lord…keep watch over your lips"* (Sirach 1:26).

The Psalm is read as a prophecy of those who plot against the Lord and judge Him. It foretells the story regarding the Jews and Caiphas. The Psalmist here sees the future Judge to be judged by sinners. But Christ overcame their accusations because in Him was nothing to be judged.

It is beginning to get intense now, the chief priests and Pharisees are beginning their plot to search for Christ so they can seize Him. If they had realised that the Lord was walking openly among them, would they had plotted to kill Him? Would Judas Iscariot set a price for Jesus, had he known that the Lord was there? As the Passover approached, and the Jews determined to put the Lord to death and knowing this, Christ retreated to a city in the wilderness called Ephraim. This is the same Ephraim in the Old Testament, which is the land where its people were fruitful. Trust that Jesus is our God, even on the Cross, where He does not have the image of a Saviour. He is our Lord even if *"there is no beauty that we should desire Him"* (Is. 53:2).

THIRD HOUR
SATAN ENTERS JUDAS

Ex. 13:17-22	Sir. 22:7-18	Job 27:16-28:1
Prov. 4:4-5:4	Ps. 41:6, 1	Luke 22:1-6

While we read about the plotting of the Jews against the Lord in the first hour, we now focus on the character of Judas. To continue our journey, in the first prophecy of Exodus we hear of the city of Etham, symbolic of the strong man who does not trust in the Lord. This foreshadows the fall of Judas because he is now in a land where fruit no longer grow, meaning that Satan has entered Judas and he is fruitless. In Sirach, the Church compares Judas to a fool and how he is worthy of death. It also tells us that the fool will be mourned for His entire life – just as today we still commemorate the error of Judas in the church, as a reminder to cling to wisdom. We briefly mention in Job Judas' betrayal, as he is the man that *"heaps up silver like dust"*(Job 27:16). Proverbs warns us not to enter in the way of evildoers or walk with the wicked as Judas did; the source of evil is in the impure heart.

> *"Thus living, let us keep guard carefully, and as it is written, "keep our hearts with all watchfulness." For we have terrible and crafty foes – the evil spirits – and against them, we wrestle, as the Apostle said, "Not against flesh and blood, but against the principalities*

and against the powers, against the world-rulers of this
darkness, against the spiritual hosts of wickedness in
the heavenly places." Great is their number in the air
around us, and they are not far from us."

+ St. Athanasius +

The Psalm speaks of Judas as the one who gathers iniquity [evil] for himself. It also exposes the excuse Judas later gives, who criticized Mary the sister of Martha, for pouring the oil on our Lord. He pretended as if he would use the money for the *"poor and needy."* These words spoken by Judas are described as *"empty"* by the Psalmist. This Psalm declares that the true blessed Lord will look after the poor, but Judas was neither.

Two common questions come up when we read of Judas' betrayal: when did Satan enter Judas, and why would Jesus pick Judas as His disciple if He knew that He was going to betray Him? Satan entered Judas when he planned in his heart to betray his Lord, and it was in this spirit that he came to the Last Supper. But after he reached for the bread, the devil no longer tempted Judas but took possession of Judas as his own. The greatest sin was that Judas was possessed by the devil's evil and trickery, instead of the Lord's love and grace.

Now, surely Christ saw His betrayal coming, right? So why did He pick Judas? Could all of this have been avoided? Satan could not have approached any of the other apostles because their hearts were steadfast and their love for Christ was immovable. Judas was in charge of the money bag and distribution to the poor, but he was greedy and a thief, so there was a place for Satan in his heart. Satan is crafty in working evil.

Whenever he gains possession of a soul, he searches for a passion that has a hold over that soul and makes him his prey. Jesus selected Judas because it was part of God's plan for salvation and for the scriptures to be fulfilled. Jesus selected him because he already had a traitorous character, and to show that even the closest friend cannot be trusted unless there is true love connecting the two. Christ even gave Judas the chance to turn to Him, to change his ways multiple times, but he still refused because he was full of greed.

Let us focus on our love for Christ today, that the desires of the world do not take hold of us so that we may continue to serve Him in fullness and not put a couple of pieces of silver in front of our Saviour.

SIXTH HOUR
BETHANY

Ex. 14:13-15:1	Is. 48:1-6	Sir. 23:7-14
Ps. 83:2, 5		John 12:1-8

In Exodus, we are reminded of how the children of Israel miraculously escaped from the hands of Pharaoh and His army when crossing the Red Sea. The cold heart of Pharaoh is compared to the warm loving heart of Moses who cries softly for the people of Israel. This reading is a type of Cross, preparing us for the Lord's sufferings. As Moses lifted up his rod to part the Red Sea and defeat Pharaoh, the Lord Christ struck Satan with the Cross and destroyed him in Hades.

In Isaiah, we read about those who hardened their hearts against the Lord's words. Despite this, God still declared to them the hidden things they have not known. He remained faithful even when they did not. Christ continued to reveal to Judas the mysteries of His resurrection and the hope it will bring, but like the Israelites, Judas had a hard heart and did not listen. Sirach also speaks of foolish deeds, remembering the sin of Judas. When the devil entered him, his wickedness became like a *"burning fire that is not quenched"* until the Lord is captured.

This Psalm contains an amazing prophecy of the conspiracy formed by Judas and the Jews against the Lord. For truly, His enemies conspired against Him in this very hour. He was preparing to institute His covenant [agreement] with His disciples and followers, they were conspiring to form their own covenant against Him. Truly, these are the enemies of Christ.

We have now reached Bethany in our journey. Bethany was known as the land of suffering and pain. The Lord comes to the land of our pain. In the first journey to Ephraim, He came to heal us from our suffering because we were dead in our sin. In the second journey, we meet Him on His way to carry our sins for us on the Cross. We see Him preparing for His burial in this Gospel as Mary offers the oil and wipes Christ's feet with her hair. Mary offered this oil as a thanksgiving offering to the Lord who raised her brother Lazarus from the dead. As she wiped the feet of the Lord, she remembered that instead of using this oil in mourning for her brother, she would use it in the burial of her Saviour. As a quick note, it is important to focus on the point that she wiped his feet with her *hair*, the honour of a woman! What great humility! The timing was perfect since she poured the oil as the rulers were conspiring to kill Christ. If she had waited one more day, she would not have received this great honour.

Having opened his heart to evil, Judas committed sin after sin, denying the covenant, stealing the treasure and finally delivering God. Sin grows in the heart, and as we read earlier in the third hour, Judas pretended to care for the poor and needy and was shocked when Mary poured such expensive oil on Christ. The fragrance of the oil symbolises the good rewards earned by a life of good works. Like Mary, we should see every encounter we have with others around us as an opportunity to serve Christ!

NINTH HOUR
THE FRAGRANT OIL

Gen. 24:1-9	Num. 20:1-13	Prov. 1:10-33
Is. 59:1-17		Zech. 11:11-14
Ps. 41:5-6		Matt. 26:3-16

There are a few prophecies in this hour but push through because it all comes together! The first prophecy comes from Exodus, and it tells us the story of Isaac's marriage. Abraham sent his servant to choose a wife for Isaac. This prophecy reminds us that the Church, Christ's bride, belongs to the bridegroom, Christ. The Church, as the betrothed to the Lord, will soon be presented to Him and united to Him through His Cross and Resurrection.

In Numbers, we see that God is upset with Moses and Aaron and does not allow them to enter the Promised Land, because they either doubted the Lord or because they struck the rock twice when our Master only struck it once. The Israelites were complaining that they didn't have any figs, fruit or water, so Moses struck the rock again to give the people drink, which indicates that Moses did not trust God enough to provide for the people. If the first strike symbolises the Crucifixion, then the second strike symbolises re-crucifying the Lord.

We read in the next prophecies of Judas' betrayal and those who are plotting to kill the Lord. In Proverbs, we read their cry, *"Let us ambush the innocent!... they hurry to shed blood...they lie in wait – to kill themselves!"* (Proverbs 1:1-25). Similarly, in the book of Isaiah we read talks of the shedding of righteous blood: *"Their feet run to evil, and they rush to shed innocent blood"* (Is. 59:7). We then read of the specific prophecy of Zechariah about the betrayal of Christ by Judas with thirty pieces of silver, which was taken from the treasury [funds] of the house of the Lord. We read this again in the first hour of Good Friday.

The Psalm simply speaks of the Lord's enemies, who speak evil against Him and devise His death. The second half of this Psalm specifically speaks of when Judas went to speak with Christ; he spoke vainly, with no love and with every intention of betraying Him. Without realising it, Judas was about to dig himself a hole he would not be able to escape from.

The Gospel reading is the same passage as the sixth hour. The same passage is read to remind us that the disciple delivered his Master. Having opened his heart to evil, Judas committed sin after sin, denying the covenant, stealing the treasure and delivering God. Judas received a lot from Christ during his three years as His disciple. He heard many sermons, witnessed many miracles, and spoke with Him often. Despite all of this, his heart did not encounter the Lord due to his love of money. How many times have we been to Church or a meeting and listened to a sermon and walked away feeling inspired? Countless! But how many times have we listened to those sermons and actually practised what was preached?

Mary, the sister of Lazarus, did not witness as much as Judas did, but she knew Christ by the purity of her heart. While greed blinded the heart of Judas and allowed him to betray his Lord, the purity of Mary's heart compelled her to pour out her love on the feet of her Saviour. Mary's anointment of Jesus is the symbol of the soul-making peace to God for the sin of the disciple Judas.

We pray that we may wash Jesus' feet with tears of repentance.

ELEVENTH HOUR
SUBMISSION AND SACRIFICE

Is. 28:16-29   Ps. 6:2, 3, 6 69:17   John 12:27-36

We have now reached Jerusalem in our journey today, the land of submission and sacrifice. The prophecy according to Isaiah speaks of the glory of the Lord and His Kingdom. In this passage, we see the Messiah coming to us in the form of the 'Cornerstone' and 'Foundation' on which the Church is built. To avoid confusion, a cornerstone is exactly what it sounds like – the corner of which two walls of a building are held together. The Bible likens Christ to a cornerstone because, in Him, the two peoples of Israel and the Gentiles are gathered together in one faith and one love. This is the same cornerstone that was rejected by Israel (1 Peter 2:6-8). The remaining verses speak of the coming of our Lord to punish the wicked, like a farmer who digs the soil and breaks it up. He appears as a gardener to us, just as He did when He condemned the fig tree on Monday.

The Psalm is a plea, a plea to the Lord so that He does not leave us alone in our troubles. David knew of the trial of physical weakness and pain; it was in the middle of his distress that he cried out to God for mercy. Sometimes, the smallest of trials can feel unbearable and we can often doubt God's love and assistance. It is in these times that we fall to our knees and seek God's mercy. This is when the second half of this Psalm comes in. When we seek God, we pray that He smiles on us and does not hide His face from us because of our weakness and our sins. So, what does this have to do with this hour's readings?

The beginning of the Gospel reading is like the Psalm we just read as it shows Christ praying and talking of His troubles, the pain He is about to go through, and the death He knows He must endure. Christ knows that He cannot escape this hour because it was for this hour that He came. The Cross was about to become a reality in the life of Christ. The voice that came down from Heaven was for the people, to reveal to them the glory of God and that this is His only Begotten Son and He will not be there much longer. God will give us every opportunity to follow Him, He will speak to us in any way He can to send us a message. Just as He did with Judas, giving him countless opportunities to turn to Him and repent, He does the same with us.

Thursday Eve
The Betrayal

Tonight, we explore the types of hearts before Christ was betrayed: the sacrificial heart, the loving heart, the hard heart, the stony heart, and the renewal of the heart.

FIRST HOUR
SACRIFICIAL HEART

| Ezek. 43:5-11 | Ps. 69:1, 13 | John 10:17-21 |

The prophecy of Ezekiel describes the wall which separates God and His people who defiled His name with their actions. This is a difficult situation in the Old Testament and brings us despair, but when we read the New Testament and the promise of the Cross, we have joy. Despite the upcoming darkness, suffering and death, God will be glorified in His resurrection. The voice of God Himself spoke in the temple of Ezekiel, showing that God's glory is active, and He is present. God Himself proclaimed that He had come back to the temple to reign. It was His throne where He would stand forever. In Ezekiel's temple, there was no division between the Jews and Gentiles, only between what was holy and what was not. This is an important fact to remember when we look at this hour's Gospel. The reason God spoke this prophecy to Ezekiel was to show him the promised temple that Israel is yet to gain which is Christ. Israel would see how great the love and grace of God was and make them ashamed of their sins. God's message to Ezekiel was that He was not finished yet. He will gather, rebuild, restore, and bring His glory!

Verse one of the Psalm shows David's distress and begs God to save him. In this Psalm, David was a type of Christ, as it begins with humiliation and ends with exaltation. When we read this Psalm, we must take notice of the sufferings of Christ, and the glory that follows. When David says, *"in the multitude of Your mercy,"* it shows that there is mercy in God, so we must take encouragement in prayer and hope in His salvation. Like the Israelites, we should look for the promised temple of God, that is our Saviour, and not have a hard heart toward His mercies.

The Lord is explaining that out of His great love and desire, He will *"lay down His life."* Remember that in the temple written in Ezekiel there was no division between the Jews and Gentiles? Funnily enough, we see that division in this Gospel! It is through the Cross that this separation is removed and we *all* enter the bosom of the Father. We focus on the power of the Lord to lay down His love – the crucifixion was not by force but out of love, which confused the Jews, causing their division between either accepting or rejecting Jesus. God the Father saw the beauty of character and self-sacrifice in God the Son, and He loved the Son all the more because of it. Anyone can lay down his life, but only Jesus could take His life up again. Because Jesus has the power to take up His own life, it is evidence of His unique relationship with His Father.

What is something you sacrifice for the ones you love?

THIRD HOUR
THE LOVING HEART

| Amos 4:4-13 | Ps. 55:21, 1 | Mark 14:3-11 |

God tells Amos that even when He blessed His people, they ignored Him. God explains how He allows so much adversity to fall on the Israelites so that they would turn to Him. He allowed rain, drought, fire, and brimstone to reign on them, but they still did not turn to Him for help. Because Israel would not listen to the Lord, His hand grew more and more heavy on them. This was not to demonstrate His anger, but His love. He starts His discipline slow and increases it so that when we turn our hearts back to Him it does not require much effort. If we do not turn back to Him, His discipline towards us grows heavier out of loving desire to see our repentance. When God says, *"you were like a firebrand plucked from the burning"* (Amos 4:11), He is saying that He saved Israel and spared them when they were at their lowest point – even then, Israel did not respond with gratitude – they did not return to God. How much He wants us to return and repent! It is because of their hard hearts that they are warned to prepare to meet their God. Because we don't know when, we must always be prepared to meet our God, especially as we face judgement.

This Psalm is the same as the one read on the first hour of Holy Thursday in the tune of *Pekethronos*. This Psalm shows David's dishonourable unnamed enemy. This describes the betrayal of Christ by His friend, the one whose *"words were smoother than oil"* but had a war waging in his heart.

Before we grieve Christ's betrayal and suffering, we, as a Church, should express an outpouring of love toward Christ. That is why we read of the love and repentance of Mary of Bethany. We see the loving heart of Mary, an example for all of us. The use of very costly oil is an example of devotion to Jesus. Often, spices and ointments were used as investments because they were small and could easily be sold; they were more than a year's wages for a worker. An alabaster flask was a small bottle with a thick neck and was opened by breaking the neck of the bottle. This Gospel suggests that Mary had poured the *entire* content of the bottle on Jesus' head. This seems very odd, but it was customary at the time to anoint the guest's head with a dab of oil. This woman poured *all* of the oil. She did this out of her love and devotion to Jesus without saying a word and without looking to others for their opinions, even though they criticised her, especially Judas. The disciples thought this act was a waste, but Jesus received it as a good work and even goes to far to say that *"she has done what she could."* God expects no more from us than what we can do. The disciples longed for fame, but it was this woman who has a lasting influence on others, not because she wanted a position, but because she simply loved Jesus and served Him. Little did this humble servant know she would be remembered forever for her small but great act of service.

At the end of this Gospel, we see that Judas agrees to betray Jesus, changing the plans of the Jewish rulers and bargained with them to give him money. For a long time, the religious leaders wanted to destroy

Jesus, now they have an ally – a disciple to betray Him.

Let us not look to the temporal glories of this world but
the everlasting glory we have promised with our Saviour.
Focus on having a loving heart for God and not for the
world.

SIXTH HOUR
HARD HEARTS

Amos 3:1-11	Ps. 140:1-2	John 12:36-43

In the third hour, we saw the outpouring love from the
heart of Mary, but in this hour, we see the opposite –
the cold, stubborn, and hardened hearts. When Israel
rejected God, He still delivered them from the land of
Egypt, proving His great love and care for them. All
through the Old Testament, God calls Israel to look back
and remember Him as the One who freed them from
Egypt. The act of redemption in the New Testament is
the work of Jesus on the Cross. In the same way, we
are called to look back and remember what Jesus did
on the cross and to live in light of that great act. In
the prophecy of Amos, we hear the warning of God
to His people against their laziness and stubbornness.
For God to speak against them shows that He must
have really been hurt by their hard hearts. The Lord
even rebukes them for their sin and warns them that
adversary shall fall on them. When Amos says, *"Surely*
the Lord God does nothing, unless He reveals His secret" (3:7),

he is speaking of the coming judgement. God revealed this secret to His prophets, and it was prophesied so long before it happened so that Israel would have every opportunity to repent. When we read about the city of *Ashdod* – the leading city of the Philistines – we read that God is inviting the nations of Philistia and Egypt to come to Samaria to see the sin of Israel. This was in order for them to understand the judgement He will bring upon the people of Israel.

In the Psalm, man is seeking salvation. We hear a cry for deliverance from evil and sin in the first verse. This is the cry the Israelites should have been saying on behalf of their sins, instead, with their hard hearts, they turned from God and continued in their evil and sinful ways. The second verse of this psalm shows that the actions of these *"evil men"* were not accidents, they were ready to start a war. Sound familiar? It should! The Jewish rulers, alongside with Judas, are these evil men who are planning their capture and crucifixion of Jesus. David goes so far to even call these men *"serpents"* because when a serpent is about to attack it licks its tongue so that the poison stings its prey when it bites. Likewise, the rulers were planning in their hearts to capture Jesus so that they could sting Him with their words and their actions so much to the point of death.

We see in the Gospel that the Jews were unable to accept Christ and hardened their hearts because they *"loved the praise of men more than the praise of God"* (John 12:43) and they feared exclusion from the synagogue. Although some of the religious believers believed in Him, they would not publicly proclaim it because they did not want to lose their position. The love of the praise of men is deadly and keeps us away from a life fully committed to God. A question does arise in this reading: why would we blame the Jews for their disbelief when God has *"blinded their eyes and hardened their hearts"* (John 12:40)? The people became blind because of their disbelief in God. They look at Him, yet do not see Him. This is the case with the sun which blinds people who have a weak vision and are unable to see its light. As to those who believe in Him and follow Him, He opens their minds and hearts to see much more. The people chose not to believe, even though Christ performed so many miracles and explained different prophecies to them that pointed towards Him. God gave them so many chances to turn to Him, just like Judas.

God reveals so much of His loving care for us in so many ways, yet sometimes we turn a blind eye and forget to thank Him. How often does it happen that we listen to God's word and forget its reality and not practice it? Through constant prayer and thanksgiving, we will be able to turn our hard hearts into loving hearts for God.

NINTH HOUR
THE STONY HEART

Ezek. 20:27-33	Ps. 7:1-2	John 10:29-38

Ezekiel speaks of the blasphemy and defilement committed against the Lord by Israel. This was the stony heart that rejected God. The Israelites offered sacrifices to their pagan gods on the very high hills and all the thick trees that God gave them! Elders originally came to seek God's word from the prophet Ezekiel. God made it clear that He did not owe any special prophecy to such a disobedient people. If we want to hear God's voice and receive His guidance, it is always best to obey what He has already said and walk in the path already revealed. The Israelites even looked for opportunities to live like the families in other countries and forsake God, serving wood and stone. We cannot serve wood and stone, we cannot go our own way. It is interesting how we speak of stones in this prophecy, look out for this in the Gospel!

The Psalm speaks of protection against enemies. When David was under attack from Cush the Benjamite, a follower of Saul, all he could do was trust God. Every other support was gone, but he needed no other support. Sometimes God's strength is evident through a trial – David was convinced that God wanted to protect him from this enemy, the one who wanted to tear him *like a lion*. This is interesting of David to say because he knows what it is like to overcome a lion; being a shepherd, he would protect his father's sheep whenever a lion or bear came and took a lamb from the flock (1 Sam. 17:34-36). As we approach the Gospel, we are slowly being introduced to the stony hearts of the Jewish rulers and Pharisees, who desire to take Christ's soul and to tear Him like a lion.

The Jews begin to take up stones to throw at Christ, but He escapes, not in panic but with wisdom. This shows the stony heart becoming a dangerous weapon. The attempt to stone Christ was not just a physical act, but a denial of His commandments. Christ explains that He and the Father are One in nature and essence. The Jews considered this to be blasphemy, but they lost this argument and could point to nothing in the words or works of Christ that showed that He was not the Messiah. Jesus prevents His stoning with Scripture, something the Jewish rulers were familiar with. The judges of Psalm 82 were called *"gods"* because they determined the fate of other men. Jesus reasoned with the rulers, would they call it blasphemy that Christ called Himself the Son of God if these judges were not called 'gods'?

The readings of this hour present the contrast between the unbelieving, stubborn and proud Pharisees that attempted to stone Christ, and the patient, wise Saviour. We think of those who once had softened hearts that became hardened over time. They no longer hear or sense God's presence in their lives. May we pray that we have soft hearts so that we do not lose our spiritual sensitivity to obey His voice and remember that the Lord is good!

ELEVENTH HOUR
RENEWING YOUR HEART

Jer. 8:4-9	Ps. 62:7, 2	John 12:44-50

Jeremiah speaks of the dangers of not receiving the Word without repentance and returning to God. If we do not repent, we remain in the state of backsliding, as was the state of the scribes and Pharisees who did not accept but rejected Him because of their hard hearts and stubborn minds. When we fall, it is expected that we get back up and return to God. This was not the case for Jerusalem; there was no sign of repentance. Even the stork, a bird with a small brain, knows how to respond to different seasons of the year. The people of God were ignorant, they do not know the judgement of the Lord; they were worse off than birds that had small brains. The people of Judah even tried to convince themselves that they were wise when they had rejected the word of the Lord, so exactly what wisdom did they have? When we reject or decide not to follow the word of God, what wisdom are we gaining? We are only gaining things that are earthly and devilish.

David trusted in God *alone* for his strength and stability. If God alone is our salvation from death, if He raised us from death to life and gave us the faith to believe in His Son, then we can take refuge in Him in trials less threatening than death! When we fall, just as the people of Judah did, we need to have the strength to pick ourselves back up and walk over to our Refuge and say we shall not be greatly moved. When we return to God, we are going home – that is the kind of wisdom the people of Judah in Jeremiah should have had in mind.

These are the last words in John's Gospel from Jesus to the public. Christ explains that He is the Light that separates light from darkness, wisdom from confusion. Yet, the Jews were still stubborn and did not understand. This speaks of trust in the Lord, for He holds even the extent of our tribulation, but also all goodness is in His hands. The Lord is asking us to renew our hearts, by shining His light upon us. If not, we will remain in darkness. Church Father St. Augustine says: "If we believe that a *Saint* has the light of God, and is enlightened in wisdom, virtue, or glory, we do not believe that it comes from him – but he is shining with Christ, Light of the world, shining in him." Unlike the people of Judah, we know to turn to God and repent, we know to reach for our Saviour and Refuge – this is the great wisdom we need to know to renew our stony hearts into loving hearts for Christ alone.

> *"The radiant angel had descended from Heaven, and rolled away the stone for those who still had stony hearts, and who supposed that the living One still lay among the dead; and had declared glad tidings to the women also, and removed their stony-hearted unbelief by the conviction that He whom they sought was alive."*
>
> *+ Eusebius Pamphlius +*

GREAT THURSDAY
The Great Sacrifice

Great Thursday is a completion of the union of the Church and Heaven. Today, we anxiously wait for the Crucifixion of our Lord and remember the last acts and words of love He gave for us.

At the beginning of the day, our Lord chooses St. Peter and St. John to prepare the bread, wine, Passover lamb, and gather other items so He may eat with them. The prayers of the first, third, sixth, and ninth hours, therefore, talk about the preparation of the Passover. 'Passover', in Hebrew, means 'to cross over', relating back to when the destructive angel would pass over the Israelites to kill the firstborn of the Egyptians. During this period, the law forbade the Jews to eat anything except unleavened bread (Exodus 12:15).

The washing of the disciple's feet. Here, we pray the 'Liturgy of the Water' (Lakan), which contains readings concerning the Lord's washing of His disciples' feet.

The establishment of the Last Supper, in which we pray the service of the Holy Liturgy. This contains readings concentrating on the New Covenant of the Holy Body and Blood.

The eleventh hour, after Holy Communion, talks to us about the piece of bread given by the Lord to Judas.

The structure of the first hour is a little different, so here is a quick rundown. After we read the Prophecies, we will chant our Paschal praise, Thok te ti gom, with the Priest, then pray the 'Thanksgiving Prayer' and the 'Prayer of Raising Incense.' The congregation then chants the 'Verse of the Cymbals.' This is the first time of the entire week that incense is raised. Even during the censing of the Church, the priest and deacon do not kiss the Cross, any icons or books. Psalm 50 is then prayed, for we are in an hour of repentance, a reminder to repent before His Crucifixion. Next, we pray the 'Litanies of the Sick', morning prayers and doxologies, and the Creed. When we recite the Creed, notice how we do not say the part about His Crucifixion – this is because the Church has not yet commemorated Christ's Crucifixion, Resurrection, or Ascension. The special hymn 'He who lifted Himself" is also chanted but in a sad tune. We will then read from the book of Acts; this surrounds David's prophecy concerning Judas and his betrayal.

Then, the deacons will chant the 'Judas Hymn' while circling the Church backwards. They even play the cymbals inside out! This is to remember that Judas had broken the law and acted the opposite way to how a Christian should. We will then chant the 'Trisagion,' 'Holy God, Holy Mighty," without mentioning the part about the Resurrection.

After, that it is back to normal until we begin the Liturgy!

First Hour
Preparing the Passover

| Ex. 17:8-16 | Ex. 15:22-16:3 | Is. 58:1-9 |
| Ezek. 18:20-32 | Ps. 55:21,12 | Luke 22:7-13 |

The prophecies in this hour combine symbols of the Cross and Passover. In the first reading of Exodus, we see the Cross in Moses' victory against Amalek only when he held up his hands in the sign of the Cross. Moses, on the top of the hill, symbolises Christ when He was crucified on the Mount of Calvary. Joshua and his men of warfighting against Amalek symbolise the challenge of the Church against sin. When Christ stretched His hands on the Cross, He embraced the whole world. When Moses held up his hands, Israel succeeded. But when he let his hands down to rest, Amalek had his chance to fight. Let us always hold up our hands with the strength of the Cross of Christ and raise our hands to praise Him.

The second reading in Exodus speaks of the tree that God showed Moses so that when he threw it in the bitter water, it turned sweet. Many Church fathers see this tree as the Cross, which works in the water of Baptism to transform our life from bitterness to sweetness. What is interesting in this prophecy is the mention of twelve wells and seventy palm trees; this is a New Testament reference to the twelve apostles and the seventy disciples. It was not enough for the people of Israel to drink from the water after it became sweet from the tree. As the Old Testament is not enough for drinking, we have to come to the New Testament and drink from the fountain of life. This idea of drink is continued in the prophecy of Isaiah when the prophet speaks of fasting. The final prophecy of Ezekiel contains the Lord's command of repentance, a life shifting from the land of bitterness to sweetness. When we look at the Cross, we should have a spirit of repentance and plead that God helps us to gain a *"new heart and a new spirit."*

The tune of the Psalm is the same as when we chanted 'Your Throne O God' on Tuesday. The same tune will be used on Good Friday as we prepare for the Lord's burial with the precious oil. The prophecy of the Psalm stresses the subtlety of the sin, as well as the extreme pain it caused the Lord, *"for it is not an enemy who reproaches me"* but a friend. This Psalm was placed in the first hour of this day to show us that the road of our salvation till the Cross cannot be combined with a person's denial or betrayal because love conquers all. We are assured here that man's denial does not prevent our salvation. God's infinite love has overcome all of humanity's corruption.

The Gospel explains the preparations of the Passover meal. As Christ is preparing for the feast, the Devil is preparing for His death. Christ had the chance to tell His disciples Peter and John about the coming betrayal, but He chose not to in order to give Judas a chance to stop His delivery to His murderers. As the Lord transformed the bitter water into sweet water in Exodus and called the people to repentance in Ezekiel, He can transform us as well as long as we willingly accept His call to repentance so that we do not become like the one who betrays Him.

THIRD HOUR
PREPARE FOR HIS COMING

Ex. 32:30-33:5	Sir. 24:1-11	Zech. 9:11-14
Prov. 30:2-6	Ps. 94:21, 23	Matt. 26:17-19

The first prophecy begins with God speaking to the people of Israel about their stiff necks and unwillingness to accept His commandments. Moses even tried to make atonement [peace] on behalf of the people by standing in between God and the sinful people. This is a symbol of the Cross. On the Cross, the Lord offered the true, eternal, and perfect atonement that Moses could not offer. It is through the blood of the New Testament that we are free. The reading of Sirach explains the might and glory of God, dwelling on high and seated in majesty. This is a symbol of His coming into Jerusalem and His high Priesthood. The breath of God spoken in verse 3 refers to our Lord's divinity as well as His Incarnation. It demonstrates that the Son was born of the Father, but was not created by Him, nor did He come after Him, but existed from the beginning with Him.

The third prophecy from Zechariah speaks of His

resurrection from the *waterless pit* with the *trumpet* blown and the *blood* of the altar. If we look at the angel that was sitting on the stone that closed Christ's tomb, it teaches us that Christ had triumphed over the closed places of the world by His power, so that He might lift us up to the light and the rest of paradise. It is through His death and resurrection that He will set us free. The prophecy from Proverbs reminds us that God is a *"shield to those who put their trust in Him."* We must trust and believe that God will protect us from every evil and will pick us up from the pits of our trials.

This Psalm speaks directly of the plotting of the death of Christ by the Jewish rulers. They know they have no evidence to support their claims of blasphemy against Christ, yet they still condemn innocent blood. The Psalm also speaks of those who seek after the righteous to bring them either into sin, suffering, or death. God allows this to happen so that He can discipline us to perfect our love which we will be able to extend even to the enemies who seek our life.

The Gospel of the third hour again speaks of the preparation of the Passover, this time from the book of Matthew. The first, third, sixth, and ninth hour gospels all speak of this same topic of the preparation for the Passover. Just as Christ is preparing for the partaking of the Passover, so are we for the partaking of Communion in the Liturgy. A question arises: why did Christ keep the Passover feast? This was to indicate in every possible way that up until the last day that He was never against the law. And why would He send His disciples to a random person? Again, to show that He could have avoided suffering, He had the power to change the minds of those who will crucify Him. So, it makes it clear that Christ is willing to suffer for everyone for the sake of their freedom.

SIXTH HOUR
PREPARE THE HOUSE

Jer. 7:2-15	Ezek. 20:39-44	Sir. 12:13-13:1
Ps. 31:18, 13		Mark 14:12-16

In the sixth hour, the Lord urges His people to repent, to help the neighbour, stranger, orphan and widow. The Lord pushes them to prepare His house so that it is not a den of thieves. Sound familiar? It should! We read about how the Lord turned over the tables in the temple in the third hour of Holy Monday. The prophecy of Jeremiah has a similar message as we read about the filth of the Jewish temple that Jeremiah calls a *"den of thieves."* The Lord had this temple destroyed and rebuilt, a symbol of Christ's forthcoming death and resurrection. In Ezekiel, the Lord also reminds us of the general sin which Judea and Israel committed, and the Lord demands that everyone return from their evil and not to defile God's name with their idols. The Lord also reminds His people of their desire to worship Him not only in the temple but on His *"holy mountain, on the mountain height of Israel."* For it is on this mountain top of worship and prayer that we will worship Him.

The final prophecy from Sirach prophesies about the enemies of the Lord who throw Him into the pit – they are unsatisfied until they shed His blood. This speaks directly about Judas the betrayer, for if he finds an opportunity his thirst for blood will never be satisfied. Very similarly to Psalm 55:21, *"the words of his mouth were smoother than butter, but war was in his heart,"* we read in Sirach that *"an enemy will speak sweetly with his lips, but in his mind, he will plan to throw you in a pit"* (12:16). Again, we are reading directly about Judas' betrayal.

Fear was on every side of King David, and he knew that whatever decision his enemies took against him, the result was not to take away his pride but his life. This was a life so valuable and useful to Israel. Likewise, in all the plots the Pharisees had against Christ, the design was to take away His life – *"They scheme to take away my life"* (Ps. 31:13). The time of life is in God's hands, not in humanity itself. We should pray with the same faith and confidence as David, knowing that God would save him. David is prophesying of those who will gather together and speak evil of the Lord. There is a day coming when the Lord will execute judgement upon them. In the meantime, we should encourage ourselves by silencing the ignorance of others and doing good in the sight of the Lord.

Christ explains to His disciples once again that they will meet a *man* carrying a pitcher of water who will show them the house where they will eat the Passover meal. Something to notice is that during this time it was women who usually carried pitchers of water, so this was a unique sign for the disciples. This house is the first Church, our Church, which is prepared for Christ's coming. The upper room was like a secret place for guests to retreat to and eat in. Jesus had reason to quietly make arrangements for the Passover. He did not want Judas to betray Him before He could give a final talk to the disciples.

NINTH HOUR
SACRIFICE AND SALVATION:
STRUGGLE AND HOPE

Gen. 22:1-19	Is. 61:1-7	Gen. 14:17-20
Job 27:2-28:13	Ps. 23:1-2	Matt. 26:17-19

This hour gives us two ironic themes: salvation must come through sacrifice, and hope is created through struggle. The first prophecy mentions the story of Abraham's sacrifice of Isaac in Genesis. This is a symbol of the Cross and the Father's sacrifice of His Son. Isaac himself carries the wood for his own death; this is a figure of Christ for He carried the burden of the Cross to His Passion. The second prophecy from Isaiah speaks of both the punishment man had as a consequence of sin and the renewal of man through salvation. When it says, *"you shall be named priests of the Lord, men shall call you the Servants of our God"* (Is. 61:6), it is implying that we as God's people have a holy occupation, namely as servants. God provides others to take care of His flocks, just as He sent Christ to take care of us.

To give a quick history outline of what we read in the next prophecy of Genesis, Abram led his army to victory over five kings. We have no idea where Melchizedek came from, or how he came to be in Canaan, or how he came to be a worshipper *and* a priest of the true God! We only know he was there. Melchizedek served

Abram bread and wine in a manner looking forward to our saving sacrifice, just as the bread and wine of Passover and the Lord's table look forward at our saving sacrifice, Jesus Christ.

The final parable used by Job explains the struggle of man in the world with the will of God. When he is cast down he questions hope in God, *"will God hear his cry when trouble comes upon him?"* (Job 27:9). God loves to restore ruins, He wants to use His people to restore and rebuild things that are broken down and ruined. This can be compared to the very special Psalm 23, which describes our Lord as our Shepherd who satisfies us all of our needs. He is the true provider of our souls as He leads us to the restful still waters.

> *"He raises, rears and feeds me on the water of Baptism, which restores health and strength to those who have lost them."*
>
> *+ St. Augustine +*

The first day of the Unleavened Bread must have been a big moment for Jesus. The Passover remembers the deliverance of Israel from Egypt, which was the main act of salvation in the Old Testament. Jesus now provides a new act of salvation to be remembered by a new ceremonial meal, something which we still take part of till this day; in fact, we are going to do it very shortly – partaking of His holy Body and Blood.

LITURGY OF THE WATER

The prayers of this hour are very similar to the funeral service prayed after the Liturgy on Palm Sunday. This act is one of discipleship, repentance, and humility. Historically, the practice of blessing water is an Ancient Egyptian practice. The early Egyptians believed the Nile River to be a source of life. This practice of blessing water gradually spread from Egypt to all Christian countries who bless water on special feast days. The Coptic Church includes the washing of the feet as part of the preparation of Holy Week as it is a sign of humility, love, and service. When Christ washed the feet of the disciples, He showed His loving service and care for all mankind; when He was crucified He showed His obedience to the will of the Father and His sacrifice to humanity.

In the ancient Coptic services, this act was performed either at the end or in the middle of the Liturgy. This was because it was customary for each person to cleanse themselves before entering the temple. For believers, this reminded them of their baptism, whereas for non-believers it reminded them of their repentance. We must wash with the tears of repentance and humble ourselves as Christ did when He washed the feet.

There are eight prophecies that we will read during this time. Why eight? It was traditionally the Jewish symbolic number of rebirth and new life since eight people were saved in the Ark. On the eighth day after birth, baby boys were brought to the temple to be circumcised. This eventually became a symbol of baptism. We will also be reading from the Pauline Epistle of 1 Timothy, as well as the Psalm and Gospel for this special Liturgical act. The readings we read this hour relate to the waters of renewal in both the Old and New Testament.

PROPHECIES

Gen. 18:1-23	Prov. 9:1-11	Ex. 24:15
Josh. 1:3	Is. 4:2-4	Is. 55:1-56:1
Ezek. 36:25-28		Ezek. 47:1-9

In Genesis, Abraham served the angels of the Lord at Mambre. He washed their feet, and then served them with bread, a calf, butter and milk. This is a symbol of the coming of Christ, who will wash the feet of His disciples in humility and service before partaking of the holy meal.

The Proverbs of Solomon points out the seven pillars of wisdom, being the seven sacraments of the Church, with the sacrament of the Holy Liturgy being one. When we read the word "wisdom" in this prophecy, swap it with "Christ. " Give it a try with the first few verses (v.1-5) – "Christ has slaughtered his meat, he has mixed his wine, he has also furnished his temple. He has sent out His maidens (servants), He cries out from the highest places of the city... "Come, eat of My bread and drink of the wine I have mixed..." Cool right? It is almost like this prophecy was written exactly for this moment. This prophecy shows the type of sacrifice, mentioning the victim, and the bread and wine. The Lord here is declaring the wine mingled with water, that it may appear as it does in the Lord's death when wine and water pour out of His holy body.

Exodus explains the Israelites crossing the Red Sea – this is a symbol of washing their feet and entering into a new land. The crossing of the Red Sea is a symbol of the water of baptism. Sin is being drowned and our salvation is being achieved. The water of the sea saved the people of Israel and drowned Pharaoh and his people. Moses' rod that separated the waters of the sea is a symbol of the Cross that abolished death. Likewise, in the reading of Joshua, we read that Joshua crossed the Jordan river completely immersed in water, a symbol of baptism. Alongside this is the prophecy of Isaiah symbolising the same thing, that this water washes away the filth of our sins. The second prophecy from Isaiah then explains the ever-lasting promise God has with His people, that He will provide for those who follow His ways. Ezekiel mentions that the Lord will sprinkle clean water to cleanse us from all the filth that has caused our sin. Finally, Ezekiel has a vision of a fountain of water flowing like a river from the altar of God into Galilee. This river contained the water of healing that would bring both life and salvation to man.

Pauline Epistle

> **1 Timothy 4:9-5:10**

In this Epistle, St. Paul explains that a good widow is one who has taken in strangers, tended to the poor, and washed the feet of the saints. Who are these saints? They are all those who are suffering. A widow should look after those who are in need, those who are not known. These widows deserve to be honoured by the Church for they wash the saints' feet through spiritual teachings. St. Paul wants women to teach godliness in the sense that they teach the young girl's purity and service. We are taught to be *"examples to the believers in word, in conduct, in love, in spirit, in faith, in purity"* (1 Tim. 4:12). This is through the act of humble and loving service!

PSALM & GOSPEL

Ps. 50:7-10	John 13:1-17

The Psalm speaks about something called *hyssop*. This was a humble plant that grew out of walls. This was used in Old Testament ceremonies as it had a special scent. It consisted of a special type of water mixed with blood for the purification of lepers. Hyssop branches were used to sprinkle the door-posts with the blood of the Passover Lamb. As we commemorate the washing of the feet, we remember Christ as the Passover Lamb.

The Gospel shows Jesus' last meeting with His disciples before His arrest. Jesus knew that His hour had come, He had lived His life for this moment and in close to twenty four hours He will hang on the Cross. This is the beginning of the end, so Christ uses these last moments to minister to His disciples by washing their feet. To wash someone's feet at that time was considered the lowest job for the servant, but Christ did not care because He loved them so much, even though He was about to be betrayed by one and denied by another.

Jesus gave Himself *completely* to washing His disciple's feet. He rose from the supper, laid aside His garments, took a towel and girded Himself, and poured water into a basin (notice how our priests will do the same thing). This was an extreme act of servanthood. Peter felt uncomfortable with this at first, but like Peter, if we do not accept the humble service of Christ to cleanse us, we have no part in Him. Although Jesus didn't *literally* wash our feet, He *did* die on the Cross to save us, and we must accept it.

Sometimes we can show a servant's heart by accepting the service of others for us. If we only serve and refuse to be served, it can be a result of hidden pride.
Anything we do for each other washes away the dirt of the world!

LITURGY OF THE EUCHARIST

The Church has completed the washing of the feet, a symbol of the purity of the people and their readiness to take part in the gifts of the Holy Spirit. It is now time to partake of the Eucharist. This Liturgy is the only sacrament celebrated during Passion Week, apart from confession.

You'll notice during the Liturgy that we do not sing certain joyous hymns; we don't read the Catholic Epistle or Acts; the Priest does not pray the Prayer of Reconciliation, and we do not chant Psalm 150 during Holy Communion; this is replaced with the prophecies of the eleventh hour of today. Enjoy the Liturgy and we'll be right back!

"Look, how the people of the Old Testament used to purify themselves to be able to eat the Passover. Moses

told them, 'Anyone who is not pure, who proceeds to eat the Passover, is perished'. How about the one who proceeds to eat the hidden mystery without preparing himself? If you cannot touch the clothes of an earthly king with impure hands, how dare you proceed to that holy sacrament with a sinful heart and impure thoughts!"

+ *St. John Chrysostom* +

ELEVENTH HOUR
THE BEGINNING OF SUFFERING

Is. 52:13-53:12	Is. 19:19-25	Zech. 12:11-14:9
Ps. 50:17-18		John 13:21-30

The reading from Isaiah is a personal message from the prophet himself. This passage explains the suffering he went through for God's people, suggesting that God accepts one's sufferings for the sake of other people. This introduces Christ's sufferings for us, as *"He was wounded for our transgressions, He was bruised for our iniquities... He was led as a lamb to the slaughter, and as a sheep before its shearers is silent, so He opened not His mouth"* (Is. 53:5-7). This reveals the mystery of the Cross and its power, as Christ stretches out His arms in love to save humanity.

This brings us to the prophecy of Zechariah, which tells us of the wounds of our Lord and the scattering of His disciples: *"those with which I was wounded in the house of my friends"* (Zech. 13:6). Although His disciples scattered after His death, they found themselves to be stronger in their faith because they were now more confident. The message from these prophecies is powerful to us as Christians as they remind us of the benefit of the true faith. Christ has taken up our sins for our sake. He suffered these things with amazing patience; how often do we deal patiently with any struggles that come our way?

> *"The teacher must suffer dangers even more than the disciple. Therefore, the devil rages with greater violence against teachers, because by their destruction the flock is scattered. By slaying the sheep, he has lessened the flock, but when he has made away with the shepherd, he has ruined the whole flock."*
>
> + St. John Chrysostom +

The Psalm speaks to Judas, who has betrayed the Lord and cast the word of God behind him. This specifically breaks the commandment of *"you shall have no other gods before Me"* (Ex. 20:3) because you are not only seeking something other than God, but you are putting something before Him. This is what Judas Iscariot did – his love of money got the best of him, and before you know it, he betrayed Christ. In the 21st century, everyone can be money hungry, but there are other things which can still have the same effects on us as they did Judas. How many times have we put social media before reading our Bibles? How many times have we put sleep first before attending a Liturgy? How many times have we put Netflix before spending quality time with God before bed? We need to know our boundaries and create a balance when it comes to these things so that we do not end up neglecting God and putting His words behind us as Judas did.

The Gospel speaks of how the Lord, regardless of all His suffering, was prepared to offer Himself as an acceptable sacrifice out of His will. He offered His life willingly. Judas' betrayal troubled Christ, but He was not taken by surprise by it because He was in control of these events. The giving of the dipped bread was usually reserved for a special guest, something like giving a toast at a wedding. It was a symbol of courtesy, so when Jesus gave it to Judas, it was a sign of divine love as well as a chance to overcome evil with good. Judas clearly did not take this opportunity to turn back to Christ because it was already in his heart to betray Jesus – he sold himself to the power of evil and greed. Judas is considered the first of the sheep to scatter from Christ, and He had not even been delivered to the Jewish rulers yet.

As we approach the Crucifixion, the number and intensity of events increase dramatically. Before we begin the final journey to the garden of Gethsemane and the Cross, we should reflect on what differentiates us from Judas, as cruel as that may sound! What do we put before God that prevents us from spending time with Him? How can we seek the Heavenly blessings before the earthly?

Friday Eve
Gethsemane

From this evening forward, the events are going to intensify. As a Church, we are collectively going to experience Christ's final moments. It is going to be emotional but remember: Christ our Saviour came and suffered for us, that He may save us through His suffering. Let us glorify and exalt His Name according to His great mercy.

FIRST HOUR
HE PRAYS FOR US

Jere. 8:17-9:6	Ps. 102:1, 8
John 13:33 – 17:26	

This hour, we add the final section to the Paschal praise: *"My Lord Jesus Christ, my Good Saviour. My strength and my praise is the Lord who became to me, a holy salvation."* This section varies in words depending on which translation your Church uses. We do this to remind us that the Lord is preparing Himself, as well as preparing us for His Crucifixion.

The prophecy from Jeremiah is moving. The Lord is explaining how the sins of His people have upset Him so much that He is to the point of tears, *"that I might weep day and night for the slain of the daughter of my people!"* (Jere. 9:1). What's interesting in this prophecy is verse 19 when Jeremiah says, *"Is not the Lord in Zion? Is not her King in her?"* Here, Jeremiah is wondering how the children of God have ended up in such a sinful state. Did God abandon them? No, Israel had abandoned God. This reminds us of Judas. He was a man of God, right? He was the most trusted of Christ's disciples, yet he abandoned God, he turned his back against Him and turned to the same sinful state. Imagine the heartache the Lord would have experienced.

This same pain is heard through the cry of David the Prophet, *"My enemies have approached me all day long, those who deride [mock] me swear an oath against me"* (Ps. 102:8). The Lord fasted, prayed, suffered, even *died* for His people, yet it does not seem that it was enough. These 'enemies' are the hypocritic Jewish rulers, who say they are God's chosen, however, they were so blind that they ended up turning against Him. The same God they praised was the same God they spat on, tortured, and crucified. We should ask ourselves, do we do the same? Do we only praise God weekly at Sunday Liturgy, going about our lives like He is not there the rest of the week? Or do we wholly give ourselves to Him and allow Him to live in us?

Yes, we are reading four Gospels each hour this evening. The Church does this so that we understand the events from the point of view of each Evangelist, as well as revealing more of Christ's final messages to His disciples. We start by reading four passages from the Gospel of John, this is the only time in the year that four gospel readings are ready consecutively from the same evangelist. This reading is a private lesson from Christ to His disciples, containing the longest prayer from the Son to the Father. In verse 21 of the third gospel reading, the Lord is comparing the Church to a woman in labour. Although she may experience pain, she will give birth to spiritual children for God. When we arrive at our final reward, after triumphing against our struggles, we will no longer remember the pain because we will be so caught up in the joy we receive.

An incredible part of the final reading is that Christ

prays for us. He prays for us so that we may not fall into the same sinful state as His people had before. Even when He was about to suffer, He still prayed for us. Yes, He still felt pain, He was human after all! How often do we get down on our knees and do the same when we are going through trials?

THIRD HOUR
GARDEN OF GETHSEMANE

Ezek. 36:16-23	Ps. 109:1-3
Matt. 26:30-35	Mark 14:26-31
Luke 22:31-39	John 18:1-2

At the beginning of Israel's history as a nation of God, God said that their disobedience and rejection of Him would bring a curse upon their land. The prophecy reveals to us that the Lord will pour out His fury on Israel for their bloodshed and disobedience, and He shall sprinkle clean water upon them. Blood and water are poured out to save His people – sounds familiar? Christ will pour out His own blood and water on the Cross so that He may save us. God's promise of restoration to Israel was for the sake of His holy name among the nations. Israel had disrespected and destroyed His name, a nation through which He was supposed to be glorified.

We see this in the Psalm, *"for the mouth of the wicked and the mouth of the deceitful have opened against me"* (Ps 109:2). Not only was the Lord betrayed by His own people, but also by those He called His disciples. Countless times, the Lord has shown love and kindness, yet this is returned with evil and He is fought against without a cause. We have all been put in situations where we are misunderstood or spoken against when we know we have done nothing wrong. It is not a pleasant feeling, so when we do it to God, how do we think He feels? When we blame God for when things go wrong in our lives or when He seems silent? He has already gone through the pain of heartbreak from His own people, His *creation*. Our King was spoken down to by His people, but He did it willingly. This teaches us two things: firstly, we should consider how we speak to others and seriously consider how we approach them with our words, and : secondly, we should not doubt God's silence, because *"the Lord was not in the wind…the Lord was not in the earthquake…the Lord was not in the fire… and after the fire a small still voice"* (1 Kings 19:11-13).

Gethsemane is an Aramaic word for 'oil press' and is also a garden in Jerusalem. Christ often went to this garden with His disciples to retreat. It is the place where Christ meets the Father, and where man betrays God. Christ had warned the disciples that they would betray Him and take offence to Him. At the same time, Judas plotted with the Jews to capture and kill Christ; out of the twelve, only eleven remained loyal.

There are two things I want you to focus on

> ### Prayer
>
> *Lord, You travelled to all these places on earth, in Hades, and in Heaven. Lord, You made it all a Heaven, for in Your presence we only dwell in the peace, love, and joy in the heavenly places. Where You are, we are, for we are abiding in You. Where You go, we shall follow.*

in the Gospel according to Mark. First is *"they had sung a hymn."* We often don't think of Jesus, singing, but He did. We can only wonder what His voice sounded like, but we know that He would have lifted up His whole heart in praise to the Father. There are three Psalms which are sung at the end of a Passover meal, Psalms 116-118. These Psalms surround prophecies of Christ's death and His work of salvation. When Jesus was on His way to Gethsemane, we can imagine Him singing these Psalms. This provides a really accurate description of how God would guide His Messiah through distress and suffering to glory. The second thing you should focus on is Peter's declaration, *"If I have to die with You, I will not deny You!"* (Matt. 26:35; Mark 14:31). Jesus knew Peter better than Peter knew himself. Peter overestimated himself, but the Lord knew he would deny Him three times and His crucifixion. This shows the reality that people will fail us, but the Lord never will. If *Jesus* suffered when He was forsaken, we can expect the same. Christ's love and restoration are greater than our failures. Come to Jesus and let it be about *Him.*

"Where are You going, Lord? Stay with us."

"I cannot for I am travelling today."

"Where are You going?"

"I am going to the Cross, then to Hades to free man from sin. Then, I will return to you for a while, but I cannot stay. I will ascend to the right hand of the Father. But do not be afraid, I will send you the Comforter until I come again."

SIXTH HOUR
CONTINUOUS PRAYER

Ezek. 22:23-28	Ps. 59:1,69:20
Matt. 26:36-46	Mark 14:32-42
Luke 22:40-46	John 18:3-9

Israel had become a land so deeply corrupted it was as if the entire land was dirty. One of God's purposes for the coming judgement was to spiritually and morally cleanse the land. In the Old Testament, the *rain* was one of the blessings a land would receive when its people walked in obedience with God. This blessing was withheld from the land of Israel because it had turned its back to the Lord. The false prophets of Israel worked together in a *"conspiracy"* where instead of serving the people, they took from them. The sin of prophets who took instead of giving was a big problem for those who promoted themselves as prophets. The priests of Israel did not take their role seriously, to serve and teach people because their lives were corrupt. An important role of the priests was that they would be able to tell the difference between something that was holy and unholy. This is a similar scenario to the Pharisees and Jewish rulers when they were judging Christ. They displayed themselves as great priests of God, but when the time had come, they took away their own King and deprived their people of the Messiah rather than serving them with Him. They had become like *"wolves tearing the prey, to shed blood, to destroy people, and to get honest gain"* (Ezek. 22:27).

The Psalm of this hour was written during a time of persecution. When Saul sent men to watch over David in order to kill him, David cried this Psalm out to the

Lord: *"defend me from those who rise up against me!"* (Ps. 59:1). This Psalm was often chanted by someone who was surrounded by persecutors, revealing a vulnerable man. We can imagine Christ in this Psalm as He prays for God's guidance in His sufferings. The Church reads this Psalm as a prayer for the deliverance of God from the hands of the evil that surrounds us.

This hour's Gospel shows us Christ asking His disciples to sit down with Him and to stay awake. He pushes them three times to stay awake and pray because His betrayers are on their way. How beautiful is it that even Christ, the Beloved Son of God, is praying during this really distressing time? At this moment, Christ has all of the power not only to encourage His disciples to stay awake and pray but also to change the minds of those coming to arrest Him. The Lord does not do these for one main reason: free will. God respects us and wants us to make decisions for ourselves, but He also wants us to make the ones that will bring us to Him; it is a compromise we can make, right? Through persistence, Christ is teaching us the importance of prayer in times of trouble. The praying in the garden of Gethsemane was from His human nature, declared by His sweat, which was from such great pain that it turned into drops of blood. This is the beginning of His suffering for us.

When we read that the Lord was sad, we must really examine everything that was said to find out why He was sad. If He knew His purpose and accepted His Father's will, then why was His soul exceedingly sorrowful, even to death? Jesus was about to be a sacrifice for our sins, and He knew exactly what was going to happen. It was not so much the physical pain that He was going to go through, it was the spiritual horror of the Cross; He was about to be made a sacrifice for *sin*. That is how corrupt humanity had become. But instead of fearing this, Christ prayed, three times to check up on His disciples, to make sure they were praying for their own strength.

How often does Christ check on us and find us asleep? It was bad enough the disciples did not watch and pray for themselves, they should have been willing to also watch and pray for the sake of Christ. This shows us the importance of prayer and companionship, being there for each other in time of need.

"He told them to 'Seep on now': and they slept, and He watched them while they slept... He said in effect: 'Go and have your sleep out; I can watch': and He watched them while they slept."

NINTH HOUR
SEIZING CHRIST

Jere. 9:7-11	Ezek. 21:28-32	Ps. 28:3-4, 35:4
Matt. 26:47-58		Mark 14:43-54
Luke 22:47-55		John 18:10-14

The mouth is a source of evil, not the mouth as an object but the way it is misused. From it comes insults, blasphemies, gossiping, lies, judgements, and sin. If you control your mouth, it will give you spiritual joy, but if your mouth controls you, you will not be able to escape its darkness. The first prophecy of Jeremiah says in verse 8, *"one speaks peaceably to his neighbour with his mouth, but in his heart, he lies in wait."* This 'one' is Judas. He kisses Christ as a friend and calls Him Master, but he betrayed the Lord in word and in deed. This is linked directly to our Psalm: *"who speaks peace to their neighbours, but evil is in their hearts"* (Ps. 28:3). These two prophecies speak of the deceit of the tongue, and that although one may speak good words, they wait to attack and betray their friend. As sad as it sounds, we do the same; get ready for a reality check! We talk behind people's backs, we can say hurtful things to people. We can also say really nice things to people and appear like sheep, but when the opportunity comes, we can plan their hurt and look like wolves.

The prophecy according to Ezekiel points to the *"sword"* that is *"polished for slaughter."* This links to this hour's Gospel as Simon Peter draws his sword and cuts the ear off the servants; yet the Lord tells him to *"return it to its sheath,"* just as it says in the prophecy of Ezekiel in 21:30. What is amazing is that Jesus is cleaning up after the disciples, healing the damage done by Peter.

The first half of the Psalm prophesies the nature of Judas who spoke in peace but had evil in his heart to betray Christ. In the second half, David declares the punishment of those who seek to kill him, *"let those be put to shame and brought to dishonour who seek after my life"* (Ps. 35:4).

Why didn't Christ escape from the Jews? His arrest does not show His weakness, it actually shows that He is our Saviour and Life. He was waiting for this moment to receive death, so He could destroy it. At the point of His arrest, all of His disciples scattered and ran for their own safety, just as He warned them. None of them stood by Jesus, fulfilling what Jesus said, *"All of you will be made to stumble because of Me"* (Mark 14:27). This shows that we never really know how strong our faith is until it is tested. Christ never once deserted His

We assume that we will be ready to stand for Christ when the day comes, whether it be a colleague at work questioning your faith, or a friend at school. There is a certain temptation to flee our Christianity when there is a cost to our obedience, and if we trust too much in ourselves, we fail. We must ask the Lord for the strength to come out strong during trials, look to Him in your time of struggle to sustain your faithfulness.

disciples, and they ran in fear of their lives at the very beginning of His sufferings. They had all been warned of the danger that was coming and even said that they would rather die than betray their Lord, yet they were seized by panic. Pain must have rushed through Christ to see this sight.

Eleventh Hour
The Trials Begin

Is. 27:11-28:15	Ps. 2:1-5
Matt. 26:59-75	Mark 14:55-72
Luke 22:56-65	John 18:15-27

The prophecy according to Isaiah speaks of the crowns of pride on the heads of the enemy, yet the Lord wears a crown of glory and beauty; this is the crown of suffering. This prophecy talks a lot about drinking. Like any other sin, drunkenness is connected to pride. Drunkenness makes everything in our lives fade away. When alcohol overcomes us, we are in sin, impairing our senses and judgement. This prophecy is trying to tell us that the drunkard needs to know that God is stronger than the drunkard, stronger than the power of alcohol, stronger than *anything*. Sometimes we see the faded glory that comes from this sin, but regardless of that, God's glory remains. Although we may lose our senses, we can receive them from the Lord. God promises that He will gather His children together from all the nations to glorify Him. This is an invitation to accept God and His promises for us. The final verse of this prophecy speaks of the rulers of Jerusalem and how extreme they were in their rejection of God; they made an agreement with death. This is like the Jewish scribes and Pharisees that were harsh in their decision to crucify Christ.

The Psalm was written during a time when there was a ceremony for a new king at the Jewish temple and royal palace. It shows how the pagan kings are against the newly anointed king. This is a symbol of Christ, the rejected King.

"He who dwells in the Heaven shall laugh at them, because the Lord indeed, being the Son, and Heir, having become Man, called those who believe in Him unto communion and participation of His heavenly kingdom and of His eternal glories. But the wicked in their pride, refused, thinking that they could reign without Him."

+ *St. Cyril of Alexandria* +

Christ is facing the scribes and elders. What is interesting is that this trial was acted out at night time. This was illegal because according to Jewish law, all criminal trials must begin and end in the daylight. Though the decision was already made to condemn Jesus, they conducted the second trial in daylight because they knew the first one had no legal standing. The efforts they went through to falsely accuse Him! There was no real evidence against Christ, the rulers could not even come up with a false testimony against Him. They charged Him with threatening to *"destroy the temple."* Little did they know that He was the temple! Through all of this, Christ remained silent. He could have called up all those He healed, those He taught; the *demons* can even testify that He is Lord. But He did not open His mouth to fulfil the prophecy, *"He was led as a lamb to the slaughter...before its shearers is silent, so He opened not His mouth"* (Is. 53:7).

The high priests spat on His face, they beat hit Him with their fists, they slapped Him with open hands. It is easy to think that they did this because they did not know who He was because they would not admit to themselves that He was the Christ; they would not admit they were not ready for Him. And on top of this, Peter denied Christ three times. God's judgement could have come down from Heaven at this point, Christ could have brought down an army of angels to defend Him. This shows the tolerance God has towards sin and the riches of His mercy. He did all of this for you.

GOOD FRIDAY

On this day, we meditate upon the Holy Cross, which is the joy of every Christian soul, the path to salvation, the road to eternal victory, the weapon against pain, sorrow, and death and the doorway to the Heavenly Kingdom. More prayers are prayed, more readings are read, and more hymns are chanted more than any other time of year. Through all of this, time really does fly.

He has gone from being revealed as the King of kings riding on a donkey to our Beloved Bridegroom to the Bread of life who offers His body and blood to us all, to finally appearing as the Lamb of God who takes away the sins of the world.

FIRST HOUR
THE TRIAL OF GOD

Deut. 8:19-9:24	Is. 1:2-9	Is. 2:10-21
Jere. 22:29-23:6	Is. 24:1-13	Wisd. 2:12-22
Job 12:18-13:1		Zech. 11:11-14
Micah 1:16-2:3		Micah 7:1-8

Well, that is a mouthful of readings! In each prophecy, you will find that the Lord promises to save His people. This glimmer of hope is shines through the Cross. As Micah, the prophet says, *"for I have fallen yet shall arise; for though I should sit in darkness, the Lord shall be a light to me"* (Micah 7:8). In the Old Testament, God often put man on trial because of his many sins and sought condemnation for his rebellion and stubbornness. The first two prophecies focus on this rebellion against God by the people of Israel. In Deuteronomy, Moses tells the Jews how they sinned against God and how Moses prayed that God would not destroy them. The Lord does not prevent us from the Cross because of our sins, no matter how great they may be.

In the prophecy of Isaiah, the Lord tells His people that they are a sinful nation who have provoked God to anger. Their troubles increase more because of their sins; but despite their sins, God has not left them. The prophecy of Jeremiah speaks of the Cross, the throne of God upon which He is glorified throughout the nations. Although the shepherds destroyed and scattered their sheep, the Lord promises that He will gather us and we will be fruitful. It is then through the Cross that the Lord converts sin into repentance, sorrow into joy. In the second passage of Jeremiah, the Lord accuses us, as His bride, of being unfaithful by having many lovers. These lovers could be the things we put before God. Despite our unfaithfulness, He still leaves the door open for us to return.

The Wisdom of Solomon shows how the Jews will examine and torture Christ, but He will be saved. They test His patience, teachings, and divinity. This was all conquered through His resurrection. The passage of Job also reveals this and refers to the Lord's victory over His enemies. Micah the prophet also reassures us of His resurrection. The remaining prophecies tell us of the trials in which the Jews falsely accuse the Lord. The Psalm of this hour specifically refers to these *false witnesses* at the trial of Christ.

Cor. 1:23-2:4	Ps. 27:12, 35:11, 12, 16
Matt. 27:1-14	Mark 15:1-5
Luke 22:66-23:12	John 18:28-40

When Judas saw that Christ was being condemned, he brought back the thirty pieces of silver, the price of a *slave*, to avoid the responsibility of innocent blood. The chief priests took the silver to buy a potter's field to bury strangers in. This was the fulfilment of the prophecies according to Zechariah (11:12-13) and Jeremiah (19:1-13). Judas hung himself, unable to acknowledge that God would forgive him, and unwilling to depend on

Christ. Instead of repenting, Judas turned one sin into another.

When Christ is returned to Pontius Pilate, he tries to release Him twice, but he gave in to the will of the Jews and released another prisoner instead, Barabbas. Pilate then washed his hands, denying any responsibility for the death of Christ. How chilling is that; the Jews would rather have had a murderer, a thief among them instead of their Messiah. What is interesting about Barabbas is that in Hebrew his name means 'son of the father'. This name represents all of us, we are all sons and daughters of the Father.

THIRD HOUR
DOWN THE 'VIA DOLOROSA': THE WAY OF SUFFERING

Gen. 48:1-19	Is. 50:4-9	Is. 3:9-15
Amos 9:4-6, 8-10	Job 29:21-30:10	

This hour's explanations will be structured a little differently, with most of the prophecies being directly compared to their Gospel fulfilment. The third hour is the beginning of the sufferings our Lord endured under the authority of the Jewish rulers. The prophecies of this hour directly speak of these sufferings. The first prophecy according to Genesis speaks of when Jacob blessed Joseph's sons, Ephraim and Manasseh. This reveals to us the mystery of the Cross and its blessing upon all the Jews and Christians that believe in its power.

The prophecy from Isaiah 50:6 says *"I gave My back to those who struck Me, and My cheeks to those who plucked out the beard; I did not hide my face from the shame of spitting."* This prophecy is fulfilled in this hour's Gospels according to John 19:3, where the soldiers mockingly say *"Hail, King of the Jews!" And they struck Him with their hands."* Our Lord is an example to teach us to bear sufferance. By His example, we can trample over all the powers of the enemy. The next prophecy from Isaiah speaks of how the children of Israel *"declare their sin...they do not hide it"* (3:9). This speaks of those who conspired between themselves to crucify Christ. In the Gospel of Matthew, the Jews cried out, *"His blood be on us and on our children"* (27:25).

The prophecy of Job says, *"they mock at me...they abhor me, they keep far from me; they do not hesitate to spit in my face"* (30:10). This is referring to the Gospel of Mark where it says, *"and they clothed Him with purple; and they twisted a crown of thorns, put it on His head... then they struck Him on the head with a reed and spat on Him; and bowing the knee, they worshipped Him"* (15:17-20). This is ironic as purple is a colour used to resemble royalty, a King.

| Col. 2:13-15 | Ps. 38:17, 22:16 | Matt. 27:15-26 |
| Mark 15:6-25 | Luke 23:13-35 | John 19:1-12 |

After Pontius Pilate sent Christ into the authority of the Jews the soldiers took Christ and paraded around Him, they stripped Him and divided His garments. This was prophesied in Psalm 22:16, *"for dogs have surrounded Me; the assembly of the wicked has enclosed Me."*

❈

Because of us, the God of Glory was stripped of His clothes, was tied to the post, and was whipped with ropes and rods in which there was a chain of bones. This innocent Body was scattered, and Bloodshed to protect us from our own wounds. By actively participating in this Holy Week, through fasting, prayer, and repentance we suffer for His sake. Suffering is a gift from God, given to us so that we can experience inner joy and strength in the death of Christ.

Through the Cross, we witness His love for us. It is in this hour that Christ is being taken to the place of Golgotha, 'Place of a Skull', and is being taken up onto the Cross. He went away from His whipping to carrying the Cross, what a scene – the King carrying the tree of punishment instead of the rod of a king.

SIXTH HOUR
HIS CRUCIFIXION

Num. 21:1-9	Is. 53:7-12
Is. 12:2-13:10	

God extends His arms on the Cross – in one hand carrying the sins of humanity, and in the other declaring the love of God for humanity, forgiveness and eternal life. Christ reconciled us with God on the Cross for our salvation. The first prophecy from Numbers introduces the *brazen serpent* of Moses. This is a symbol of the Cross, crushing

Satan and all death – *"when he looks at it, shall live"* (Num. 21:8). We must believe in the power of the Cross as it acts as our cure and victory against sin. The second prophecy from Isaiah also speaks of the powerful sign of Christ as the Lamb who is brought to the slaughter. In the Jewish tradition, lambs used for the temple sacrifices were born in Nazareth, fed in Jerusalem and slaughtered at Golgotha. Isaiah 53 foreshadows Christ's death as it tells us of the crucifixion, burial, and inheritance of salvation, which is also reflected in the prophecy of Isaiah 12 where it speaks of the day of salvation being a day of joy; *"therefore with joy you will draw water from the wells of salvation"* (Is. 12:3). Both Isaiah and Amos prophesied that the sun will be darkened during His crucifixion, revealing to us the hidden glory of the Cross; *"I will make the sun go down at noon, and I will darken the earth in broad daylight"* (Amos 8:9).

Gal. 6:14-18	Ps. 38:21, 22, 22:16, 17, 18, 7, 8
Matt. 27:27-45	Mark 15:26-33
Luke 23:26-44	John 19:13-27

After the prophecies, we read from St. Paul's letter to the Galatians. The theme of this reading is 'the glory of the Cross'. During the time of His crucifixion, the Cross was considered the worst type of way to die and was reserved for the worst criminals. The point of placing the individual on the Cross was to not only bring them shame as they are raised in front of everyone but to remind the people what their death could look like if they were found guilty of a major crime. Christ's "crime", or accusation, was blasphemy, claiming that He was God. When He hung on the Cross, two thieves were hung with Him. This is a true mockery because He was considered a curse, *"cursed is everything that hangs on a tree"* (Deut. 21:23). To some, the Cross was a shameful thing, but to us as Christians the Cross is the highest form of glory, as St. Paul says, *"God forbid that I should boast except in the cross of our Lord Jesus Christ, by whom the world has been crucified to me, and I to the world"* (Gal. 6:14). The second half of this verse is stating that by accepting His Crucifixion and the Cross He has carried for us, we are dead to the world and are alive in Him. The Lord loved us so much that He took it upon Himself to be considered like those He was being crucified with that we may have this life in Him.

The Psalm speaks directly about the piercing of Christ's hands and feet on the Cross. While David was writing this Psalm, he was struggling against his enemies, at the same time describing the wounds of the crucifixion that his Great Son would bear. In his crisis, David was the focus of unwanted attention and his tormentors did not allow him to suffer quietly or privately, rather exposing him to everyone. Christ also found no place to hide from the unwanted stares of the cruel, mocking men at the Cross. David was so powerless against his enemies that they took even his clothing and used it for themselves. Christ was not only stripped completely naked, but the soldiers even gamble with His clothing at the foot of the Cross; *"They divided My garments among them, and for My clothing they cast lots"* (Ps. 22:18).

When Christ was about to breathe His last, *"from the sixth hour until the ninth hour there was darkness over all the land"* (Matt. 27:45). We recreate this scene in the Church by turning off all the lights and only seeing the light of the Cross. The beaten Lord is dressed in a scarlet robe, a purple cloak, and a crown of thorns, and a reed is placed in His right hand. Bending their knees, the people mock Him. Having taken our sins with Him, He is covered with our scarlet blood, but He is cloaked with the honour of the prophets and patriarchs in purple cloth. He is crowned with thorns, being pierced and struck with the former sins of the Gentiles. While He was hanging from nails upon that Cross, He prayed to His Father for us. Even now He still prays for us!

Prayer

Your Body is torn by whips and I wear nice clothes, living lavishly and carelessly. You are given myrrh to drink, and I enjoy the desires of life. You comfort my pains and sufferings and I refuse to repent. I ask You to have mercy upon me, for I know how tender Your overflowing mercy is.

He could see all His enemies, those who betrayed Him, those who were raging at Him, but He was still praying. They were saying "Crucify Him!" but He was saying *"Father, forgive them for they do not know what they do"* (Luke 23:34). In the Gospel of Luke, we read of the first person guaranteed entry into Heaven, the right-hand thief being crucified next to Him. We can often doubt our worthiness and place in Heaven, but when we declare the words *"Remember me when You come into Your Kingdom"* (Luke 23:44), He surely will.

Through all this pain and humiliation, while He is being mocked, He is being adorned.

Ninth Hour
His Death

Jere. 11:18-12:13 Zech. 14:5-11 Joel 2:1-3:10-11

This hour is the most climactic and overwhelming time the Church experiences. We are looking at our Bridegroom hanging on the Cross and at His greatest act of love for us. This is our Salvation, our power over death, our sins forgiven, our lives renewed. What a breathtaking moment.

The first prophecy from Jeremiah prophesies about the Jewish rulers who make a plan to kill Christ and remove Him from this earth by means of the wood of the Cross, *"they had devised schemes against me, saying. "Let us destroy the tree with its fruit and let us cut him off from the land of the living"* (Jere. 11:19). Our Lord is that sweet fruit being cut off from its tree, it's home. It's interesting to think that those who put Him to death could think that they kill the only source of life. From this moment on, death has a new meaning: life eternal.

The next prophecy from Zechariah announces that *"the Lord shall be King over all the earth"* (Zech. 14:9). Although His death on the Cross was real, He remains alive as we chant together with the Angels the Trisagion, "Holy God, Holy Mighty, Holy Immortal". This prophecy reveals how far His Kingdom will reach, like the overflowing waters from Jerusalem for all who come to drink, Jew or Gentile. God will be declared the King of the whole world by everyone from every nation.

| Phil. 2:4-11 | Ps. 69:1, 2, 21 | Matt. 27:46-50 |
| Mark 15:34-37 | Luke 23:45-46 | John 19:28-30 |

The reading of Philippians explains the cry of the Lord, which we will read in the Gospels. When the Lord willingly and humbly *"emptied Himself and took the form of a servant"* (Phil. 2:7), He accepted the shame and death on the Cross where most of humanity abandons Him. During this time, the Father never abandoned His Son. Instead, the Lord glorified Him, accepted His sacrifice as a sweet aroma that was pleasing to Him. God did all things through Christ; He became a slave so that He could share human suffering in the flesh.

When the Lord cried out that He was thirsty, the soldiers gave Him vinegar soaked in a sponge on a spear. This is prophesied about in the Psalm, *"and for my thirst, they gave me vinegar to drink"* (Ps. 69:21). It was probably this same spear that was used to wound Christ. The spear had supposedly entered from His right side ending in His heart. This was mentioned in Psalm 109:21, *"My heart is wounded"*, literally. The soldier who struck Christ with this spear was named Longinus. After witnessing the blood and water that poured out of Christ on the Cross, he confessed that Christ was indeed the Lord and became himself a martyr. How amazing, the Cross is so powerful that it even changed the heart of someone who had to confirm Christ's death. When we sin, we are like this soldier, striking Christ another time in His heart. But we are all called to repentance, no matter how big the sin.

Jesus knew great pain and suffering in His life, both physical and emotional. He was betrayed by His friends, He was beaten and spat on by His own people, He was mocked, and now He is being crucified. Through all of this, Christ had never known separation from His Father, now He does. Jesus felt forsaken by His Father at this moment and cried out, *"My God, My God, why have You forsaken Me?"* (Mark 15:34). This Psalm was written when King David was being hunted down by Saul and his own son; he had felt that God left him at such an intense time of his life. Christ had done nothing for His Father to forsake Him, but that's where it gets interesting; God never once forsook His Son. This cry was a declaration to the people to show that He was, in fact, fulfilling a prophecy one last time, *"My God, My God, why have You forsaken Me? Why are You so far from helping Me, and from the words of my groaning?"* (Ps. 22:1). Was this Christ's humanity crying out? Probably, but this scene reveals to us that it is possible to feel alone in moments of great suffering. We've all experienced it, even Christ did. There are times when we can feel lonely and we have no one to talk to, no friend to call, no one to hang out with. But God is always waiting, He is waiting for you to talk to Him about what's bothering you. He wants to hear about your day, why you feel frustrated and alone. We must remember, that God did not leave His Son to hang on a Cross, He used Him to collect His children from Hades and to resurrect!

God never forsakes His children, He loves us too much.

ELEVENTH HOUR
BEING TAKEN DOWN FROM THE CROSS

Ex.12:1-14	Lev. 23:5-12

In the first reading of Exodus, we read the story of Moses striking the rock in the desert, out of which sprung water that quenched the thirst of the Israelites crossing the desert. Previously, in the ninth hour, the Lord thirsted. He reminded us of the thirst which He mentioned to the Samaritan woman. This Living Water is the water of salvation: *"the water that I shall give him will become in him a fountain of water springing up into everlasting life"* (John 4:14). When we have a taste of it, we will never want anything more. In our lives, the Passover is of great importance similar to baptism. Just as the waters of the Jordan saved the Israelites from the evil army of Pharaoh, so does the baptismal waters save us from Satan's forces. Once the Jews crossed the waters, they began a new life, just as we did the moment Christ was crucified on that Cross. The crossing of the Red Sea by Moses and the Israelites is also considered as the *"Lord's Passover"* (Ex. 12:11). Similar to Moses when he had parted the waters and crushed Pharaoh's soldiers, Christ had destroyed the soldiers of Satan at the bottom of the sea. Moses used his staff, Christ used the Cross. They both stretched their arms out like an eagle. The Psalm of this hour echoes this desire to be saved, *"rescue me and deliver me out of great waters"* (Ps. 144:7). Another prophecy is echoed in this Psalm – the end of the struggle and sacrifice of our Lord. In this hour, we will meditate on the final words spoken by the Lord, *"it is finished!"* (John 19:30). This is the Lord's declaration that all of His promises have been fulfilled for humanity. After He declares this, the soldier Longinus pierces His side, and blood and water come out from His wound. This declares two essential truths for Christians – that we are saved by both His blood on the Cross and the water of baptism.

Gal. 31-6	Ps. 144:6-7, 31:5	Matt: 27:51-56
Mark: 15:38-41	Luke 23:47-49	John 19:31-37

The gospels speak to us of His sacrifice. Christ opened up His arms the whole day for our entire life. His blood pours out of His wounded side, a sign of the promise He has made for us which takes us from death to life. The water cleanses us and grants us purity, peace, and love. These are the fruits of the Spirit given to us through baptism. The blood of Jesus will dye our hearts as a sign of our salvation when we share the Cross with Him.

How crazy was His death? The earth shook, the rocks split, *graves* were opened. But what was even more amazing was the women that were serving Him; Mary Magdalene, Mary the mother of James, and the mother of Zebedee's son. These women were the most inclined to feel for Christ, to grieve over His sufferings. How amazing is their dedication! They had followed Him to the Cross, ministering to Him wherever He went. They had witnessed every event – how He wept, how He gave up His Spirit, how the rocks were split, and how He was taken down from the Cross. The women were the first to see Christ at His death and burial. When the disciples fled, the women were still there – what courage! St. John Chrysostom says of this:

"Let us men imitate the women, let us not forsake Jesus in temptations... there is no difference whether you give to Him, you have nothing less than these women that then fed Him."

TWELFTH HOUR
THE BURIAL

Lam. 3:1-66   Jonah 1:10-2:7

The prophecy from the Lamentations of Jeremiah is a long one. In a beautiful tune, the Church cries out its lamentation for Her Beloved. In this hour, we see the Holy Mother of God carrying the Lamb of God, we see Joseph and the women anointing the Holy and Pure Body with spices for burial. *"My eyes overflow with rivers of water for the destruction of the daughter of my people. My eyes flow and do not cease, without interruption, till the Lord from Heaven looks down and sees"* (Lam. 3:48-50). This is the cry of the Church, weeping with the holy women, the daughters of the city. The Church sings from this book as it is full of prophecies of the Lord's burial, foreshadowing the descent of our Lord into Hades to free Adam and Eve from the bondage of sin. Jeremiah tells us, *"I called on Your name, O Lord, from the lowest pit. You have heard my voice"* (Lam. 3:55). The Lord hears us in every place, but especially now, He has descended into the lowest pit to lift us up from our sin, giving us the power of His soon Resurrection. God never hides His ear from us. When you are in the pit and cannot speak when you cannot cry, be still. God can understand everything because He has been through everything.

We all know the story of Jonah inside the great big fish. Inside the fish, Jonah entered into death to discover the mystery of Christ's Resurrection which is victory over death. In the fish, Jonah gave us a beautiful song of praise which expressed Christ's redeeming work during the moments of His death on the Cross and His burial, *"You have brought up my life from the pit, O Lord, My God...Salvation is of the Lord"* (Jonah 2:6, 9). Jonah knew God heard his prayer before the answer came. God can give us total peace and assurance that our prayers are answered before the actual answer comes. The Church reads this prophecy to show us the similarity between Jesus and Jonah as they both remained concealed, rising after three days.

Ps. 89:6, 23:4, 45:6, 8	Matt. 27:57-61
Mark 15:42-16:1	Luke 23:50-56 John 19:38-42

The Psalm of this hour shows the royal Bridegroom at His eternal throne. Not only do the words *"Your throne, O God, is forever and forever"* (Ps. 45:6) specifically refer to Jesus, but also that God the Father regards Him as the eternal heir to His throne in His Kingdom. His Kingdom is filled with righteousness, the natural result of His love. The final verse of this Psalm is also a direct reference to Christ's burial, *"Your garments are scented with myrrh and aloes and cassia, out of the ivory palaces, by which they have made You glad"* (Ps. 45:8). These sweet and beautifully scented spices were used in the burial of Christ, smothering His garments as He was placed in the tomb.

It was Roman conduct to leave crucified bodies on the crosses for the birds to peck at. The Jewish would throw the bodies in a pit where garbage and sewerage were burnt. Joseph of Arimathea requested that Pilate let him take Christ's body to a tomb. Nicodemus helped Joseph with this as well as helping supply the perfumes and pure linen for His Holy Body. They wrapped the Body in long stripes of linen and treated it with a mixture of spices. Something beautiful about this is that Mary the Mother of God and Mary Magdalene were at the tomb waiting to anoint the Body. What courage! How deep is their affection for Christ?

Let us imitate these women; let us not forsake Christ in times of trial. These women exposed their lives so much for Him while He was alive, they were ready to die for Him as well. When He gave His life for us, these women committed themselves to take care of His Body.

Bright Saturday
Khristos Anesti!
Christ Is Risen!

There are no words to describe this night, it is a beautiful personal experience. No one can express the joy of this night but you.

Yesterday we were crucified with Christ, today we are glorified with Him.

Yesterday we died with Him, today we are given life.

Yesterday we were buried with Him, today we rise again with Him.

He lifted us in His Resurrection.

We ask that He lifts us up forever.

We lived in darkness, He gave us light.

We lived in sin, He gave us holiness.

We dwelt in sadness, He gave us eternal joy!

CPSIA information can be obtained
at www.ICGtesting.com
Printed in the USA
FSHW022309080222
88187FS